ADOPTED
by the
KING

Cynthia Johnson

ISBN 978-1-63525-531-7 (Paperback)
ISBN 978-1-63525-532-4 (Digital)

Christian Faith Publishing, Inc.
296 Chestnut Street
Meadville, PA 16335
www.christianfaithpublishing.com

Printed in the United States of America

Preface

The theme of this book is about a child's love for her father and her heart desire to receive that love returned back to her. The theme of the Bible is about a King and his Kingdom. The heart desire of the King is all his kingdom people will love and receive him. Unfortunately many choose to reject him.

When I was rejected and abandoned for no fault of my own by my physical daddy, my (and yours) spiritual daddy was, has, and always will be, here offering true, deep, can't even wrap your mind around it, unconditional love for his child.

In this physical realm, many of my choices were made for me.

In the spiritual realm, the King allows His children to make their own choices.

The life changing choices of his kingdom people lead them to destruction or victory. In the Bible you will discover the true experiences about real people who have journeyed before you. How awesome it is to have a King that loves you so much, that He provided His Word and His only begotten Son as an example to follow.

How your life story ends, depends on choices you make as you travel through this physical realm. We all have the same Heavenly Father. He promises to never reject or abandon you. Do you know your true daddy? Are you willing to turn to Him and allow him to teach you how to live a life pleasing to him?

The whole purpose of this book is to share with others what I discover for myself. I was never alone. My true daddy was always with me. I have been adopted by the King of all creation.

Contents

I Did Not Know God, but God Did Know Me

Genesis 1:1–4 King James Version: "In the beginning God created the heaven and the earth. And the earth was without form, and void; and darkness was upon the face of the deep. And the spirit of God moves upon the face of the waters. And God said, Let there be light: and there was light. And God saw the light, that it was good; and God divided the light from the darkness."

Psalms 139:11–18: If I say, Surely the darkness shall cover me; even the night shall cover me; even the night shall be light about me. Yea, the darkness hideth not from thee; but the night shineth as the day: the darkness and the light are both alike to thee. For thou hast possessed my reins: thou hast covered me in my mother's womb. I will praise thee; for I am fearfully and wonderfully made: marvelous are thy works; and that my soul knoweth right well. My substance was not hid from thee, when I was curiously wrought in the lowest parts of the earth. Thine eyes did see my substance, yet being unperfect; and in thy book all my members were written, which in continuance were fashioned, when as yet there was none of them. How precious also are thy thoughts unto me, O God! How great are the sum of them! If I should count them, they are more in number than the sand: when I awake, I am still with thee.

My name is Cindy, I am the second child born to a teenage mother (Ellen) and a young father (Don) in the early 1960s. My parents divorced before my fifth birthday. My mother too inexperienced for the responsibilities of rising babies, and went her own way to figure life out. My father became a single, hardworking man of two small and very needy children. In the beginning, my older brother Steve and I spent most of our time in the care of our grandparents (Daddy's parents). They lived on a farm so Steve and I had adventure and our imagination soared. Steve and I did everything together. My mother would visit with us, but never stayed long. Daddy met and married a woman named Kara, who soon gave birth to my baby brother (Bobby). Daddy purchased a small house, moved Steve and me in, and together we became a family unit. Kara insisted Steve and I refer to her as Mom. I was told not to call her husband Daddy anymore, because according to Kara that was to intimate. And Kara told Steve and me, "Your mother gave you away for a piece of furniture, she does not want you, and you are never allowed again to speak of our mother." In those young and impressionable years I soon forgot all about my birth mother. During the summer months, Steve and I would go with Daddy to Okoboji Lake, where he had a restaurant. We would help him in the morning preparing and serving the meals. Then he would let us play down by the water, giving stern instructions not to go beyond the point, where he would not be able to see us. Daddy rented a cabin and we went to the fairgrounds at night, riding all the rides. Because Steve and I were only one year apart in age, we both had the same physical size body frame, and we both had blond hair, and bright green eyes, people often mistook us for twins. People would approach Daddy and make comments about how cute his children are. Daddy would smile, puff out his chest with pride, thank them and always reply, "They look just like their mother." I enjoyed spending this time with Daddy and Steve and getting all this attention from strangers. Kara and Bobby were not with us, so I asked Daddy why. Daddy said, "Bobby is too young and at home with his mother."

The persuasive power is in the story, not the storyteller. God's way of thinking is not like the world's way (normal human wisdom). And God offers eternal life, which the world can never give. We can spend a lifetime accumulating wisdom and yet never learn how to have a personal relationship with God. We must come to Christ to learn this important truth. Christ's death for sins sounds foolish to those who don't believe. The "foolish" people who simply accept Christ's offer are actually the wisest of all, because they alone will live eternally with God. No amount of human knowledge can replace or bypass Christ's work on the cross. If it could, Christ would be available only to the intellectually gifted and well educated, not to ordinary people or to children. To receive salvation is so simple that any person who wants to can understand it. Skill does not get a person into God's kingdom (simple faith does) so no one can boast that his achievements helped him secure eternal life. Salvation is totally from God through Jesus's death, which made us perfect in God's eyes. There is nothing we can do to earn our salvation; we need only to accept what Jesus has already done for us. God is the source of our relationship with Christ. That relationship is personal and living. Our union and identification with him results in our having God's wisdom, possessing right standing with God, being holy, and having the penalty for our sins paid in full by Jesus.

God is omnipresent—he is present everywhere. Because this is so, you can never be lost to his spirit, and his character goes into the creation of every person. He is with us through every situation, in every trial—protecting, loving, and guiding us. God makes no mistakes, he has a plan and a purpose for everyone, and God knew ahead of time into whose care I would be placed in, what I would go through, and in his perfect timing how he would reveal himself to me.

During my childhood I was raised in a quiet little town. Uncle Dale would stay with our family often. Dale had many physical disabilities. He had been born with polio, therefore he was crippled in both his legs, had no teeth and could not speak well, but God had given Dale a quiet, gentle soul and he loved all of us kids.

One of my fondest memories as a child was going on what Dale called the long walk all around the town. Steve and I would push our infant brother Bobby in his stroller as Dale walked beside and watched over us. This walk took about one hour. There was one school for age pre-K through twelfth grade. There was a grocery store, a hardwood store, a bank, a bar (that I was not allowed to go in) a diner, and a library that Dale and I visited as often as we could. The streets were lined covered by huge beautiful oak trees and in the backside alleys there were tons of fruit trees. Mulberry, plum, apple, pear, and cherry just to name a few. Dale would encourage Steve and me to eat as much fruit from these trees as we desired. Sometimes we would even venture onto someone's personal property, climb up into the trees for the best fruit on the branches. We would climb up the trees, throw the fruit down for Uncle Dale to catch and climb back down. Dale would bring out of his pockets a large variety of all the fruit we had collected along the way, pull out an extra blanket from Bobby's stroller and prepare a fruit picnic lunch under the shade of the tree branches. Dale encouraged Steve and me to eat until we were stuffed. No one ever got mad at us for this behavior and sometimes the owners of the home where the fruit trees were growing would bring us out a peanut butter and jelly sandwich to add our picnic. In spite of Dale's physical limitations, his love and concern for the children entrusted into his care was top priority. Through Uncle Dale, I learned that our identity, value, and worth come from God. I didn't understand at the time, but looking back now, I believe Uncle Dale to be an angel sent by God to watch over me. *I did not know about God, but God did know me.*

Psalms 91:11–12: "For he shall give his angels charge over thee, to keep thee in all thy ways. They shall bear thee up in their hands, lest thou dash thy foot against a stone."

One of the functions of angels is to watch over believers (Hebrews 1:14). There are examples of guardian angels in Scripture (1 Kings 19:5; Daniel 6:22; Matthew 18:10; Luke 16:22; Acts 12:7) although there is no indication that one angel is assigned to each believer. Angels can also be God's messengers (Matthew 2:13; Acts 27:23, 24). Angels are not visible, except on special occasions (Numbers 23:31; Luke 2:9). It is comforting to know that God watches over us even in times when we as children have no knowledge of him yet.

Our family was poor, but so was everyone else in town, so we fit right in. The community offered for free many opportunities to come together to enjoy family ordinated things. Most of these events were connected to the small white Lutheran Church located near our home, but we never attended that church or any other events the community offered to the family. Growing up with a family that was disconnected from the community and the church was both confusing and challenging. As a child, I had no knowledge or understanding of the spiritual realm, but I could see the church from my bedroom window and often wondered about the families attending. An outing for our family consisted of putting on shorts, going to the park, swimming in the lake without Daddy present. When I asked Kara, "Where's Dad?" She said, "He is working hard to provide for this family's needs." I believe Daddy loved his entire family equally and to the best of his ability, he provided a comfortable home, food for our bellies, and clothes for our physical bodies. The area in life that needed leadership and healing for the entire family was our spiritual life.

Hebrews 10:24–25: "And let us consider one another to provoke unto love and good works: not forsaking the assembling of ourselves together, as the manner of some is; but exhorting one another: and so much more, as ye see the day approaching."

In life a child's first teacher is the parent and the parent's first priority should be to teach and instruct the children in the way of the Lord. A parent cannot teach what they have not yet learned for themselves. The church provides a meeting place where families can come together to receive encouragement, and help in the growth process as the people strengthen each other in faith. Difficulties in life should never be an excuse for neglecting church attendance.

Matthew 6:24: "No man can serve two masters: for either he will hate the one, and love the other; or else he will hold to the one, and despise the other. Ye cannot serve God and mammon [money]."

Jesus says we can have only one master. We live in a society where many people serve money. They spend their lives collecting and storing it, only to die and leave it behind. Their desire for money far outweighs their commitment to God and spiritual matters. Jesus contrast heavenly values with earthly values when he explained that our first loyalty should be to those things that do not fade, cannot be stolen or used up, and never wear out. Jesus is calling for us to make a decision that will allow us to live contentedly with whatever we have because we have chosen what is eternal and lasting.

While in the early years of my life I remember being treated differently than my brothers. Kara would make me go to my bedroom right after supper, before Daddy got home, and tell me not to come back out. She would use her tone of voice and words in a threatening way toward me saying, "If you disobey me, you will not ever see your father again." In fear I obeyed her, remained in my room and often wet on myself as I slept during the night. I very seldom was allowed to spend any time with Daddy. When those cherished moments did happen, Daddy connected with me through our love of chocolate. Daddy would always buy me a dish of ice cream with double layers of hot fudge and tell me, "Now don't you tell your mom I did this, she might get jealous." Daddy called me his little princess and often made the statement, "You look so much like your mother." Not having memories of my birth mother, I would look at Kara, thinking to myself, what is Daddy talking about? I don't look anything like her. My physical frame was very thin. I had long skinny legs and thick, curly, blond hair. Often people would comment about how beautiful my hair was. I knew Kara loved her baby more than me, but I thought it was because he was the baby. I did not understand why Kara did not like me.

When I started kindergarten, Kara had all my beautiful hair cut off, put me in a short dress, and made a diaper out of an old dishtowel for me to wear. I cried and begged her not to, but she told me when I grow up, stop wetting the bed, and stop acting so prissy, she would allow me to grow my hair and wear regular panties like other girls. She continued saying, "And since you act like a boy, you may as well look like a boy, maybe when your friends tease you for wearing a diaper, you will stop peeing on yourself." I believe my teacher intervened on my behalf, she put regular panties on me, and when I got home after school, Daddy was yelling at Kara. Daddy was scolding her for cutting my hair and saying, "How dare you, putting her in a diaper and embarrassing my child like that." Kara tried defending her actions saying, "I cut her hair because she got cockle burs (spikey weeds) in it and I could not comb them out. (This was true, I did get cockle burs in my hair, but I didn't need to get *all* my hair cut off and I was never allowed to grow my hair back out again.) As far as putting me in a homemade diaper—Daddy would accept no excuse to justify that action, Again I say, *I did not yet know God, but God did know me.*

Ephesians 6:1–3: "Children obey your parents in the Lord: for this is right. Honor thy father and mother; which is the first commandment with a promise; That it may be well with thee, and thou mayest live long on the earth."

There is a difference between obeying and honoring. To obey means to do as one is told; to honor means to respect and love. Children are to obey while under their parents care and children should honor their parents even if the parents are demanding and unfair. Adult children are not asked to be subservient to their domineering parents and children are not commanded to disobey God in obeying their parents. During this season of my young life, I had to learn how to survive—obey and submit to the authority God had placed over me.

Hebrews 13:17: "Obey them that have rule over you, and submit yourselves: for they watch for your souls, as they must give account, that they may do it with joy, and not with grief: for that is unprofitable for you."

At around age ten, I recall overhearing several arguments between Daddy and Kara. The first one I remember is when Daddy received the call that his mother had passed away. Kara told Daddy if he attended his mother's funeral she would leave him and he would never see his baby, Bobby, again. Daddy did not attend his own mother's funeral. Years later, my birth mother, told me she did attend my grandmother's funeral in hope she would see Don and be able to reconnect with Steve and me. My mother said she was disappointed, but not surprised when Don did not show, because Kara always answered the phone, never allowed her to talk with Don concerning her children, and had repeatedly been told by Kara, "Steve and Cindy belong to me now, and as long as I have authority over them, you will never again be allowed to see your children." Another fight between Daddy and Kara was concerning Steve. Kara was saying she could not stand being around Steve any longer because according to her, he was being disrespectful and defiant. From that moment on Steve would go to work daily with Dad, and I was left alone (with my little brother) under the supervision of Kara. Separated from the protection of my older brother and the loving care of Daddy, life as a child became even more difficult for me. Although, I'm sure, there were many circumstances surrounding the situation of my biological mother that I was not aware of—interfering between the communication of the adults, concerning the health, safety, and welfare of their children, in my opinion, is downright evil.

My stepmom taught me how to work very hard. I had to get up at 4:00 a.m. to clean the house, do the laundry, and cook breakfast for the family. Kara gave me the orders and would go back to bed. Around 6:00 a.m., Kara would come out, tell me to go to my room and not to come out until she told me to. I could hear the conversation at the table as the rest of the family enjoyed breakfast. My daddy would ask, "Where is my little princess this morning?" Kara's answer was always the same, "She is in her room primping, I will make sure she has something to eat before she goes to school." After Daddy left for work, Kara would call me out of my room, and if I was lucky I might receive a half grapefruit or a piece of dry toast (I was never allowed to have jelly or even butter on the toast). I say if I was lucky, because most times, I was sent off to school on an empty stomach. When I returned home from school, in the heat of the day, I was forced to work in the garden. I would ask for cold water to drink, but was only allowed to drink the lukewarm water from the garden hose.

If I tried to run the water long enough to get it cold, from the house, Kara would scream, "Stop wasting all that water, it's your fault, your dad has to work so hard to pay for these bills."

During the harvest time, I would spend hours upon hours gathering, washing and preparing the vegetables for freezing or canning. Most nights I would prepare supper for the family, given a small amount of food for myself and told to go to my bedroom before my dad arrived home from work. Again, able to hear the conversation, Daddy would praise Kara for being such a great wife, who kept a clean house, tended the garden, and always prepared such a great meal. Whenever Daddy asked about me, Kara always laughed, saying, "Oh, your little Cinderella is in her room studying." Daddy would laugh at that comment, but I'm sure he thought, because my name is Cindy, Cinderella was a nickname of loving endearment that his wife attached to me. Little did my daddy realize, that his little princess was in fact, being treated cruelly by the evil stepmother.

Kara constantly reminded Daddy of my struggles in math, how often the teachers had to call me out for talking in class, and how my desk had to be moved away from the window so I could stay focused on what was being taught in class. I did have these weakness—math, talking, and daydreaming. My favorite thing to do was read. I loved a good book, and since I spent most of my childhood in my bedroom, I would read for hours anything I could get my hands on. I had a very active imagination and as I read, I could travel all over the world and visit all sorts of faraway places in my mind. I dreamed of my future I hoped for, and imagined what my life would be like when I would be set free from Kara's authority over me, and I dreamed of being allowed to spend quality time with my daddy. Reading was my way of escape from reality and of the pain and confusion I was experiencing. *Yes*, I became a dreamer (a big one), and *yes*, I became a talker (a big one). I did not understand why I was getting disciplined for this behavior, I had found something I could do really well. I could talk. Later in my life, what my parent's viewed as a weakness, God viewed as a strength and would use my nonstop ability to talk for his glory. *I did not yet know God, but God did know me.*

Colossians 3:20: "Children, obey your parents in all things: for this is well pleasing unto the Lord."

Our family moved to Kansas City when I was twelve years old. With this move Daddy's relationships with his side of the family were completely severed. Being disconnected from my cousins, teachers, and childhood friends I had grown to love was challenging enough but the idea of attending a new school in the big city was exceptionally fearful for me. This would have been a great time to get a good book in my hands. The Bible.

Teenage years are difficult for most, and I was no exception. I still had the very thin physical frame, long legs, and my breast had not yet begun to develop, in fact I had absolutely no curves at. Being a late bloomer is devastating for a teenage girl, and I was such a girl. Kara made me clothes out of her old garments to wear to school. Kara is at least three times my size, had short stocky legs, and very large breast. All her clothes were of polyester fabric. This very large material was stretchy with old outdated designs on it. Kara cut, sewed, and tried on me these items she was creating. Somehow Kara did manage to get her old clothes to somewhat fit me. The creation was like a one-piece jumpsuit. Because of my long legs, the crouch area fell around my knees, and because of my flat chest the seams for the breast area were at my waist area. I looked absolutely ridiculous. For gym class, shorts, a white T-shirt, and tennis shoes were required, with the option available of a gym uniform. Kara bought for me the gym uniform and simple white slip-on shoes.

I still had the short boy haircut (this time frame is during the seventies when girls wore long hair), and personal hygiene products were not provided for me. When my monthly period started, I did not have a clue what was happening to me. Scared out of my mind, I told Kara about the blood I saw in my underwear. Kara told me that only dirty, nasty women have periods, and since it was happening to me, I must be a whore. She told me to put tissue in my underwear and I perhaps the bleeding would stop. Filled with shame, I did as I was told. The last thing, I thought to myself, is for anybody to know about this shameful thing that is happening to me. I told no one and asked no questions because I did not want anyone to know I was labeled a whore.

This of course continued happening monthly with more blood and included intense sharp pains in my stomach. I continued using toilet paper to keep the blood from getting on my clothes. Kara noticed the large amounts of toilet paper being used and told me I was allowed to use only two squares from now on. So when my period started the following month, I took an old rag usually used for dusting with me to school, washed it out in the bathroom sink between classes and used it to absorb the blood. One of my friends saw this, asked me what and why I was doing it. I told her my shameful secret of being a whore. My friend told me the truth about what I was experiencing and explained that it happens to all girls around this age. Angry, and for the first time, I yelled at Kara for lying to me. Smiling and laughing at me, Kara said, "I was wondering how long it would take you to figure it out. You are so stupid."

The following month, Kara handed me one Kotex pad to wear during my period and at the same time said, "I want to see for myself how much blood you are flowing, and when I feel it is appropriate I will give you another pad." Because I did not have a heavy blood flow, Kara would not give me a fresh pad. Around the third day, I was able to smell myself. I started collecting the blood from hamburger or chicken packaging and when I was in my bedroom at night, I would pour enough blood on the pad to where it would be justified by Kara that a new pad is needed.

I continued this behavior for several years. Although I requested pain medicine for the cramping, it was never provided. In time, I purchased my own pads and pain reliever. I kept these items in my gym locker at school and during the summer months, I hid the items from Kara at my friend's house. *I did not yet know God, but God did know me.*

My older brother Steve was treated in a similar way. Steve had a very thin body frame, all his hair was shaved from his head, and after working all day with Daddy, Kara would time Steve's showers, giving him only two minutes to clean himself. Kara shopped for Steve's school clothes at an area thrift store. Kara must have searched for

ADOPTED BY THE KING

hours, finding the ugliest outfits she could find. All of Steve's pants had wild designs, and when he tried them on, they fell to his feet. Kara punched holes in one of Daddy's old belts, handed it to Steve, and told him to make the pants fit. Steve argued with Kara but did as he was ordered. Steve also looked ridiculous, with his pants all bunched up and his belt twisted several times and tied in a knot around his skinny waist.

Bobby, Kara's own son, also would be attending a new elementary level school. Bobby's physical body frame was husky and thick. Bobby had blond hair, wore it shoulder length, and he was allowed to style his hair anyway he choose. As a child, Bobby was allowed to play outside and often got covered in dirt. Kara bought Bobby great smelling bubble-bath and lots of tub toys. Bobby would splash and play for hours with his toys in the tub. When he finished his bath (usually when the water became cold), he looked like a wrinkled prune, and smelled fresh and clean. I went with Kara as she shopped for Bobby's school clothes. Kara gave special attention in choosing just the right items. Kara told me she did not want Bobby to be teased because of his chubby midwaist and she needed to choose clothes that would camouflage this area. She also purchased for Bobby the most recently updated fashion of tennis shoes. Bobby always got anything he asked for.

Some people might think I should be jealous of this drastic and painfully obvious difference in the treatment Bobby and I were receiving from Kara (remember, at that time I thought Kara was my mother also), but I never recall having any bad feelings toward my little brother. Deep down inside of me I knew, Bobby did not know what his siblings were experiencing at the hands of his mother. Although I had no understanding of why this was happening in my life, I did know, it was by no fault of Bobby. I loved being a big sister to my little brother, and I still do today. *I did not yet know God, but God did know me.*

John 13:34: "A new commandment I give unto you, That ye love one another; as I have loved you, that ye also love one another."

I dreaded my first day of school at the junior high level. I thought because of my appearance and smell, I would not be accepted by my peers. Upon arrival at school the first place to go was the assigned homeroom, where the students received instructions on school etiquette, locker assignment, and class schedules. I searched the room looking for a place to sit and finally spotted a seat in the far back corner. I sat down and took in the atmosphere. Most of the students were laughing and talking about the great summer adventures they had shared together with their family. Nobody seemed to notice me and I felt relieved inside. The first class on my schedule was home economics, the second was gym, and so on. I was thrilled with this schedule. With economics first, I would be able to eat. And with gym second, I would be able to shower afterwards using hot water and soap. Being provided with food on my stomach and being clean and smelling fresh I would be able to succeed well in the rest of the classes. Math class was after lunch. Again, great! *I did not yet know God, but God did know me.*

I was disappointed to learn that in economics, sewing class was to be accomplished during the first semester, and cooking would be during second semester. My teacher (Mrs. White), however, took a special interest in me. The second week of school, Mrs. White pulled me aside and said, "Cindy, if you come to class as soon as you get off the bus, I will have a surprise for you." Happily, I agreed to see her before doing anything else. My surprise the next day, and every day following was a muffin, apple slices, and orange juice.

The class was given a note to give to our parents, instructing to provide material and a pattern for our first project. I gave the note to Kara, who went to the thrift store, buying for me some ugly material and an outdated dress pattern. When Mrs. White asked the students to share with the others about the materials and the outfit they were going to make, I sunk down in my chair. All the other students were thrilled and excited about what they were about to make. Mrs. White looked at my items, smiled and said, "You should feel very lucky, I'm going to be able to teach you how to modify an old, outdated pattern into a beautiful dress, and I have some left over material in the cabinet that should be just the right size for you." With her help, I choose the perfect material, redesigned the pattern, and was very proud of the finished project. Of course, I never took the dress home, but I did put it on and wore it at school. I loved my economics class, and I loved Mrs. White. *I did not yet know God, but God did know me.*

The other class I enjoyed the most was gym. I was the only student in class who wore a uniform, everybody else had cute short outfits and nice tennis shoes. So when I got home one night, I sneaked into my little brother's room and stole a pair of his shorts, T-shirt, and his brand-new shoes. I was a girl and five years older than him, but his clothes fit me well. Bobby's shoes were tight. I had to curl my toes to squeeze my feet in and it hurt when I walked, but I did it. Kara did not miss the shorts and shirt, but she did ask what happened to his new shoes. I pretended not to know, and I did know Kara would replace the shoes for Bobby.

As I cleaned house in the morning before school, I would collect the change from under the cushion of Daddy's chair. Daddy lost lots of quarters, dimes, nickels, and sometimes fifty-cent pieces. I gave the money to a friend at school and she bought for me items I needed for personal hygiene, such as deodorant, shampoo, toothbrush, toothpaste, and a few pieces of makeup. I also acquired some hair gel and with the help of my friends, we tossed and fluffed my short hair until it looked somewhat stylish. I kept these items in my gym locker at school and after I showered, I would put on a little makeup. I always combed out the hair gel and removed the makeup before going home. One time I didn't get off all the mascara, Kara saw it, and slapped me silly. I excelled in English class. Once I wrote a paper, my teacher submitted it in the school fair and I received a blue ribbon. I was so proud of the blue ribbon, and I thought to myself, this will be put on the fridge, Daddy will see it, and maybe Kara will stop being so hard on me concerning my low math grades. When I got home, Kara took the paper, waded it and the ribbon up and threw them in the trashcan. Daddy never was told of this accomplishment in my life. Kara said she would take away all my books if I did not spend more time on my math.

Math was then and always has been a weakness of mine. At Christmas time, I got tons of dot-to-dot coloring books and many math related flashcards. Kara would set a timer and go through the math cards demanding I give her a correct answer. In one hand she held the flashcards, in the other she held a short piece of a yellow garden hose. When I was unable to give a correct answer before the timer went off, she would call me stupid and hit me with the hose. I would cry, begging her to stop hitting me, and when that didn't work, I would just stand still refusing to say anything at all. Kara then would tell me to say something, anything, even if it is the wrong answer. Kara would beat on me for hours, and at the same time, smiling, laughing and saying to me, "You are so stupid that you would rather get beaten than say something." I believe that it was in this moment that I realized I would never please Kara. Daddy seemed blind to the abuse and Steve was unable to protect me. I felt I was in a no win situation at the hands of my abuser. I was broken down, I didn't know how to fix the problem, and I simply wanted to give up on trying. I kept hearing this voice inside my head repeating—don't give up, don't give up—someday you will do great things! I did not know where that voice was coming from, but I agreed with that voice in my head saying, "*I am not stupid!*" *I did not yet know God, but God did know me!*

I enjoyed going to school. I always smiled and gave a nice complement to every one of my fellow students, so very few teased me about my clothing. When someone did try to bully, laugh, or make a commit about my outfits, my friends defended me. Other students were not as fortunate as I was in resisting the bullying. I distinctively remember four girls. Cindy was teased for being overweight. Bobby Jo was teased because of her braces. The twins, Colleen and Collet were teased because they had bad eyesight and had to wear thick, pop-bottle style glasses. These castaways and I became great friends. We sometimes would talk about the pain of being bullied and feeling like nobody accepted and loved us. We encouraged each other often. School breaks were always difficult for me because I was not allowed to talk on the phone or make any contact with my friends. To protect myself, I withdrew from everything, casted my I eyes downward, stopped caring about my grades, and stopped listening to others that were trying to encourage me. I felt unwanted and unloved. At times, I contemplated suicide. Deep down inside my gut, I knew suicide was exactly what Kara wanted me to do. But again, inside my head

I heard that voice telling me not to let her win. Then she would be freed by my bad choice. I didn't know where these thoughts were coming from, but again I became determined not to quit. I kept telling myself, I do have a future beyond Kara's authority over me, and I want to experience it. Again I say, *I did not yet know God, but God did know me. And He was watching over me!*

Matthew 18:1–6, 10–14: "At the same time came the disciples unto Jesus, saying, Who is the greatest in the kingdom of heaven? And Jesus called a little child unto him, and set him in the middle of them, and said, Verily I say unto you, Except ye be converted, and become as little children, ye shall not enter the kingdom of heaven. Whosoever therefore shall humble himself as this little child, the same is greatest in the kingdom of heaven. And whoso shall receive one such child in my name receiveth me. But whoso shall offend one of these little ones which believe in me, it were better for him that a millstone were hanged about his neck, and that he were drowned in the depth of the sea.

"Take heed that ye despise not one of these little ones; for I say unto you, That their angels do always behold the face of my Father which is in Heaven. For the Son of man is come to save that which is lost. How think ye? if a man have one hundred sheep, and one of them be gone astray, doth he not leave the ninety and nine, and goeth into the mountains, and seeketh that which is gone astray. Even so it is not the will of your Father which is in heaven, that one of these little ones should perish."

I continued to spend time with Mrs. White. One morning while eating the breakfast she provided for me, she sat down and asked me about my personal hygiene issue. She said, "I noticed when you get to school, you often smell of urine, do you have a bladder control problem you would feel comfortable sharing about with me?" She continued, "I'm only asking because many times bladder problems can be controlled with the right medicine." I trusted Mrs. White and told her the truth. For the first time in my life, I told of the conditions in which I was living at home. I told her, "I'm not allowed out of my bedroom after my daddy gets home from work. I smell of urine because I use the trashcan in my room to relive myself.

I'm only allowed to shower once a week and I can't wash my hair because Kara keeps the shampoo in her bedroom. I'm not allowed to use deodorant or shaving cream and razors and I've started developing pubic hair."

"See," I said, raising my arms up so she could see the hair growing in my armpits.

1 Thessalonians 3:12: "And the Lord make you to increase and abound in love one toward another, and toward all men, even as we do toward you."

Galatians 5:14: "For all the law is fulfilled in one word, even in this; Thou shalt love thy neighbor as thyself."

Love is such a powerful word. It is one of the strongest emotions a person feels, but love is much more than a feeling, it is an action.

The next day at school, I was called to the counselor's office. A man and a woman asked me many questions, like where do you sleep and eat at your home, where is the bathroom located in your home, and have you ever had a doll. I answered all their questions honestly. I told them, "I sleep in a small room in the basement, the bathroom is located upstairs, in the hallway next to the rest of the family's bedrooms, and the last time I had a doll was (after a long pause) I can't remember." They told me to go back to class and they would talk with me later. During the last hour in school, over the intercom, I was called to return to the office. The same man and woman from earlier were waiting for me and asked me to go with them to the hospital to get checked out. The office staff reassured me that it was okay to go with them, stating "We have been given permission from your father to release you into their care." I was admitted into the hospital and subjected to all sorts of tests. They seemed especially concerned about the scars on my back and shoulders. I told them, "I really don't remember how I got them, all I can tell you about the burn scars, is what I've been told about them. I was told that while I played around the stove at my grandmother's house, I accidently hit the handle on a pot of boiling water, tipping it over on myself. I was just a baby at the time." They seemed satisfied with that explanation. The nurse then put a needle in my arm and hung a bag of fluid from a hook by my bed. I asked what it was and she told me nutritional stuff. "Why do I need that?" I asked. She replied, "Because you are malnourished and underweight." I responded, "I've always been skinny." The nurse smiled at me and stated, "There is a big difference between being skinny and being starved." I stayed overnight at the hospital. The next day the phone in my room rang. I started not to answer, because Kara never allowed me to answer or talk on the phone at home. Afraid it might be Kara on the other end ready to scream at me for answering the phone, I quietly picked up the receiver and said, "Hello."

A voice I did not recognize said, "Cynthia, this is your mom, how are you feeling?" Confused I asked, "Who are you?" "Your mom, your real mother Ellen, do you remember me?" I responded, "My mom's name is Kara." There was a long pause then Ellen continued, "Your father and I were married before he met Kara. Steve and you are my children." Just then Kara and Daddy walked into the room. Scared out of my mind, that Kara caught me on the phone, I made eye contact with her, extended my arm, handing her the phone. "She says she my mom," I blurted out. Kara took the receiver and slammed it down on the phone. Daddy, seeing the puzzled look on my face, told me the caller must have had the wrong room.

A few days later, I pulled my brother Steve aside and quickly told him about the phone call I received at the hospital. "She said she is our mom, yours and mine," I explained. Surprised that I didn't know, Steve told me about our mom and made me promise not to say anything to Kara. He then asked, "Do you remember that time when Kara and I were arguing and she pushed me down the steps?" "Yes," I replied. "Well," he continued, "that's when I told her to stop beating on you and making you cry. I told her I was going to kick her m——f——ass if she didn't stop. I got in trouble for cussing and Dad believed her instead of me. Kara convinced Dad to take me with him to work every day and I have been working ever since."

I asked Steve how Daddy treated him during the day. Steve said, "Dad's great, I'm learning all kinds of cool stuff. Dad said he would start paying me for helping him when I get older. I worry about you though, how are you doing with the old bitch?" I thought for a moment then answered, "I'm learning how to survive!" Steve gave me a loving smile and finished the conversation with a statement. "Now that you told someone, maybe Dad will believe what I've been telling him along." I thanked Steve for telling me the truth about our mother and promised him I would not let Kara know about this conversation. Although Steve was only one year older than me, he trained, prepared, and encouraged me with his words, and how to function in this season of my life without him. In my heart I believe God purposely designed my life by giving me this older, stronger, and wiser brother. I love Steve for trying to protect me. *I did not yet know God, but God did know me.*

Isaiah 3:12: "As for my people, children are their oppressors, and women rule over them. O my people, they which lead thee cause thee to err, and destroy the way of thy paths."

Parents are responsible for leading their children. It was disheartening for Steve and me to experience these confusing emotions concerning our parents. Kara was cruel and wicked toward us and it seemed Daddy was completely blind of this fact. God's Word says parents will be held accountable for how they led their children. If you are a parent, you must lead according to God's just commands.

I was released from the hospital back into the care of Kara and Daddy. When I arrived home, I noticed many things had been changed. The first thing I noticed was the location of my bedroom. My room was no longer in the basement. A room previously used by Kara for office space had been beautifully redone for me. I had a brand-new canopy bed with matching dresser and nightstand. There was a bookcase filled with all kinds of age appropriate books I could read. A record player, easy-bake oven, and a Baby Alive doll with clothes and bottles were also provided for me. I was twelve years old, but I was thrilled, it had been a long time since I had been given a doll. Daddy told Kara to take me shopping and to get me some clothes like other girls my age wear. Jumping up and down with excitement and grasping at the opportunity, I quickly made eye contact with Daddy and begged, "Can I please have jeans, Daddy?" "Yes, sweetheart," he replied, "you can have jeans." Giving Kara a stern look, Daddy said to her, "Get her some jeans, and get Steve some jeans too!" Kara and I went shopping at a real clothing store. Kara allowed me to pick out my own tops, but she put polyester pants in the cart for me. Boldly, I stated, "Dad said I could have jeans like the other kids!" Kara gave me an evil look and said, "Your dad's not here now, you will get what I pick out for you." Like an afterthought, she muttered, "I guess you can get one pair of jeans." I wore the jeans almost every day to school, changing out the tops. Although we had never attended church, I had seen what the other kids wore to church on Sunday. The other clothes Kara bought for me looked like church clothes. Steve also got some new clothes. Most of his shirts were button-down with collars, unlike Bobby's shirts, which were sporty. At least the clothes fit us, and both Steve and I were happy with the new clothes.

Lots of other things changed also. In the morning, Daddy would cook a big breakfast with eggs, bacon, french toast, etc., and I was allowed to have jelly or syrup on the bread. Steve and I took showers in the morning and we were provided with personal hygiene products. I informed Daddy that my period had started. He gave me a concerned look and said, "Well, I'll take you to the store, but you got to get that stuff for yourself." From that moment on I kept my personal hygiene items on a shelf in my room. I no longer had to request Kotex pads from Kara and whenever I needed more things, I told my dad and he would take me shopping.

Daddy worked during the day, while Steve and I were at school and most nights he was home for supper. I was fed well, allowed to watch TV with the rest of the family, and around 9:00 p.m. before I was sent to bed I relieved myself in the bathroom, therefore, I no longer needed to use the trashcan in my room. Daddy told me, "I will leave the light above the stove on and I put a nightlight in the hallway so you can find your way to the bathroom should you need to go during the night." I thanked Daddy for the extra efforts in the lighting he put into place for me, but to the best of my recollection, I slept peacefully throughout the night. Daddy started picking Steve up from school to take him to work and I stayed after for math tutoring. My math grade went from an *F* to a *C* (at least I was passing), and Daddy always took the time to look at our grade cards. Most of my grades were *B*s with the exception in English class, there I always received an *A* plus. Daddy would give us cash allowance for the good grades and tell us to try harder on the lower grades. Most times Daddy would take us out for ice cream to spend the allowance. Sometimes he would tell us to save it for something we might want later on.

I caught the late bus home from school after tutoring. I would be alone with Kara and my little brother for a couple of hours before Daddy got home. During that time frame, I work outside in the garden area, collecting the fruits and vegetables. I mowed the grass, cleaned the fence-line of weeds and pulled up dandelions. I also had to vacuum the swimming pool daily. It was very hard work in the hot sun and I was not provided the right tools. Without gloves and in short pants I was made to squat or kneel down (could not sit, or Kara would scream at me for being lazy), and use a pair of old scissors, a fork and butter knife to remove the weeds from the yard. I really did not mind doing these chores because I knew when Daddy returned home, if the work was already done, he and I would be able to spend some time together. Learning to keep a positive attitude during this season in my life was difficult, but not impossible. *I did not yet know God, but God did know me.*

One day after Kara had given me her orders, she packed up Bobby and was at the grocery store when a new neighborhood kid, my age, saw me working in the yard and stopped to talk with me. This nice looking black boy's name was Byron. He asked me if he helped finish the yard work, could he take a dip in the pool. I told him, "I have to clean the pool first and I was not allowed to swim it in until Daddy got home later but I was sure it would be okay." Byron mowed the lawn while I tended the flower gardens. Together, we got done earlier than normal, so I told him, "See you tonight," and went inside to start the laundry, dishes, vacuuming, dusting, etc. That night after supper, with the rest of the family, I went swimming. Daddy was picking all of us kids up and throwing us in the water. I was having a great time and had forgotten to tell Daddy about my new friend, so when Byron arrived in his swim trunks, I quickly told Daddy how he had mowed the lawn and I had invited him back for a swim. Daddy said, "The lawn looks great, thanks for helping my daughter, jump in and cool off." We played for a while and when Byron left for home, I told him, "See ya tomorrow at school."

That night Kara and Daddy had another argument. This time it was about Byron. Kara was screaming at Dad, saying, "I can't believe you allowed that nigger to swim in our pool. Don't you know that our property value is going to go down now, with them living in the neighborhood. And what's even worst is that nigger saw your daughter in her swimsuit. Black people grow up to be child molesters and I do not want the other neighbors thinking bad about this family." I listened as Daddy told Kara about how wrong she was, but from then on, I only spoke with Byron at school. I told Byron of the argument between my parents, stating, "I'm so embarrassed and sorry, I've never heard the n-word spoken before in our house." I continued saying, "Daddy has many black friends and they come over all the time." Byron said he understood and he would still be my friend. Again I say, *I did not yet know God, but God did know me.*

Matthew 7:1–3: "Judge not, that ye be not judged. For with what judgment ye judge, ye shall be judged: and with what measure ye mete, it shall be measured to you again. And why behold the mote that is in thy brother's eye, but consider not the beam that is in thine own eye?"

Having a judgmental attitude that tears others down in order to build oneself up is a byproduct of a negative thinking lifestyle. Jesus tells us to examine our own motives and conduct instead of judging others.

Daddy's main source of income was made by installing furnaces and air conditioners, but he also worked some nights at an area ice rink repairing the mechanisms under the ice. During the summer months and on weekends Daddy would take all three of us kids to the rink, put us in ice skates and let us learn how to skate. At first we all just pulled ourselves around the rink holding on for dear life to the outer rail. In a short amount of time, Steve was doing okay, in my opinion, I was doing much better than Steve, but not near as good as Bobby. Bobby, five years younger than me, didn't appear to be afraid of falling at all. Wobbling out to the center of the rink and doing all kinds of crazy turns he quickly became a natural on skates.

Dad and Kara made the decision to pay for hockey lesson for him. It was exciting watching my little brother blossom in this area. I was very proud of my brother and looked forward to watching his hockey games. In the stands I would barely sit down before I was standing up and cheering for him. Steve also played hockey one season, starting at a later age, Steve was not as experienced as some of his teammates, but he did okay. I loved watching my older brother, just as much as watching my baby brother. In the stands, Kara would sit next to me. Kara would go wild when Bobby got the puck and made a shot. Bragging to the other people saying, "That my son." She did have a reason to be proud, because Bobby was very good. I however, loved both of my brothers, and her attitude toward Steve was embarrassing. When Steve got the puck and made a shot I went wild, giving Steve the two thumbs up jester. Kara would just sit still doing her needlepoint that she had brought with her. The people around would say to her, "Look, isn't that your son? Did you I see what he just did, aren't you proud of him?" Looking down at her needlework, Kara would laugh and say something like, "Oh, I've got more important things to do, than watch him make a fool out of himself or boldly proclaim, 'He. Is. Not. My. Son. My son's name is Bobby." She then diverted any recognition Steve might deserve to the accomplishments Bobby had earned.

Bobby always got brand-new and the safest equipment available and Kara made sure his ice skates were always sharp and laced up very tight for good ankle support. Steve had the needed equipment for the sport but his was hand-me-downs, worn out by other players. One night Steve got hit in the face with another player's hockey stick. The stick went through his face mask and split open his forehead. Steve was bleeding very badly. I jumped up along with all the other spectators and ran down to the rink to see how bad my brother had been hurt. The referees were telling Steve not to move so they could check him out. Then I heard Steve say, "Help me off the ice, I'm okay." I gave a sigh of relief, and looked around for Kara. I looked up into the stands and spotted her, still sitting there and working on her needlework. Steve got several stitches in his face but healed up well.

I also skated. I wore figure skates and watched how the other girls held their arms for balance, placed their legs for twist and turns and quickly self-taught myself. One night a lady talked with Daddy saying, "I've been watching your daughter, who is her coach?" Daddy told her I didn't have one. The lady looked at me, smiled big and said, "Let me coach her, she has great potential." Daddy asked about the fee and told the coach he would let her know. That night, I overheard Kara and Daddy arguing over money again (this was a common argument between Kara and Daddy). Kara's voice was very loud, and I was sure Steve could hear also and maybe Bobby. Kara yelled, "Steve and Cindy are your problem, my concern is for Bobby only. It is your fault for having these kids, not mine. I have only one child. You expect me to take care of your kids and share with them what should belong only to Bobby. If you want them to have extra activities and waste your money on them, you are going to have to work harder. You need to make a decision about who is most important. My son will not go without, because of your children." The next day, I talked with Steve about the argument. He said he heard it to. I told Steve I didn't want Daddy to work harder, because he already works too hard and I would rather have Daddy home with us. Steve agreed with me and said he would tell Dad tomorrow at work. Steve finished out his one season in hockey, I never got figure skating lessons, and Bobby as always got it all.

During the summer months Bobby also played baseball and Daddy put me gymnastics and baton. My classes were held at the high school and offered to kids for free. With my skinny, limber body, I excelled on the mats in tumbling, the uneven bars and the balance beam. Because of these learned skills, when school started back up, I tried out for the spirit drill team, and made it. I got very skilled in twirling the baton and was asked to perform at the school games, but was not allowed to. According to Kara, the school uniform that parents were required to buy for the student, was way too expensive and showed way too much of my body. I also earned patches, had pictures taken with my classmates, and was awarded trophies for my accomplishments. None of these items were ever purchased for me. Many pictures and trophies of Bobby's progress were throughout the house, but there were never any pictures of Steve or me in the house. For Christmas cards and other special occasions, family pictures only included Kara, Dad, and Bobby. Other items that represented milestones of accomplishments in childhood years like, yearbooks, class rings, or letterman jackets were never purchased for Steve or me. Steve to the best of my recollection never did extracurricular activities again after his hockey accident. Steve was only allowed to go to work daily with Dad.

1 Corinthians 3:11–15: "For other foundation can no man lay than that is laid, which is Jesus Christ. Now if any man build upon this foundation gold, silver, precious stones, wood, hay, stubble; Every man's work shall be made manifest: for the day shall declare it, because it shall be revealed by fire; and the fire shall try every man's work of what sort it is. If any man's work abide which he has built thereupon, he shall receive a reward. If any man's work shall be burned, he shall suffer loss: but he himself shall be saved: yet so as by fire."

A building is only as solid as its foundation. Two sure ways to destroy a building are to tamper with the foundation or build with inferior materials. Good work will be rewarded; unfaithful or inferior work will be discounted.

"He himself shall be saved; yet so as by fire" means unfaithful workers will be saved, but they will be like people escaping from a burning building. All their possessions (accomplishments) will be lost.

The foundation of our life is Jesus Christ; he is our base, our reason for being. A parent must build their children's lives with high-quality materials (right doctrine and right living) that meet God's standards. When a family or home is built on Jesus Christ, each member will become mature, spiritually sensitive, and doctrinally sound.

Our home was filled with those whose work was "wood, hay, and stubble." Kara was immature and insensitive to the needs of all the children for which she had taken responsibility for and Daddy didn't know how to take leadership and was unbalanced in his responsibilities.

Several years later, I asked my birth mother about Daddy's spiritual life while they were married. She told me, "Your father and I took you and Steve to church every Sunday and your father was very close and active with his family members. After church, we always went to your grandmother's for a big family dinner together. Your father said he gave his life to the Lord when he was a child."

Hebrews 10:23–24: "Let us hold fast the profession of our faith without wavering; (for he is faithful that promised;) And let us consider one another to provoke unto love and good works."

We have significant privileges with our new life in Christ:

1. We have personal access to God through Christ and can approach him at any time.
2. We may grow in faith, overcome doubts and questions, and deepen our relationship with God.
3. We may enjoy encouragement from one another.
4. We may worship together.

I did not yet know God, but God did know me. And God had given me a daddy who believed in him. My daddy had just forgotten "who he is in Christ."

Many more years will pass before Daddy remembers "Apart from Christ, you are nothing."

Escaping Captivity
but Still in Bondage

Our family moved often. At around age fifteen we moved again. Daddy now owned his own heating and cooling business and Kara took care of the record keeping concerning the business. I just assumed the family relocated in order to be closer to the business. Daddy hired someone to keep up the lawn work, so my main responsibility was to care for my ten-year-old little brother and keep the house clean. Bobby and I got along great with each other and I also received permission to watch two neighborhood boys after school and received $5.00 per week for doing so. Most days Kara would pick up Bobby, taking him with her, so I had only the other two. This was good because without Bobby at home, I often watched cartoons with the other boys. When Kara got home in the evening, she expected all the cleaning of the house to be completed. Bobby was at an age where he would slip up and tattle on me for watching cartoons instead of working on the house.

We lived within walking distance from a roller rink, so with the money I earned for babysitting, got permission to go skating. This request was granted by Kara; with the condition I took Bobby and watched over him. Bobby didn't enjoy skating much, so I bribed him to go by promising him the money I had earned for the game room arcade. Many of my classmates from school would also be at the rink, so my social life greatly increased. One of my guy friends from school had a job as the rink guard. He noticed that I didn't have my own skates, so he gave me a pair of his old ones. Since he was a guy, the skates were black and very well worn in, but they were good quality. In time, I used some of my money to replace the jumpers, the stoppers, and the wheels. I also purchased skate covers and pom-poms, giving my skates a female appearance.

We began to do couple dancing on skates together and attracted a lot of attention. I learned how to do on roller skates everything I was not allowed to do on ice skates because Kara did not want Daddy to pay for the coaching. I had a great time. Kara never came to the rink, if she had, and seen me having a good time, I'm sure she would have put a stop to it.

One day while I was cleaning the house, Kara came back home early and picked up Bobby to take him school supply shopping. Since I was not finished with the laundry yet I asked to stay behind and begged her to let me go skating when I was done. *She agreed!* I tell you the truth, I just about fell over. Kara had *never* allowed me to be alone in the house before or go by myself to do something I enjoyed. She told me to make sure to lock the door when I left, and she would be home when I returned from skating. I quickly finished the laundry, grabbed my skates, locked the door, and ran to the rink. When I returned home, Kara was not there, so I sat down on the front porch steps and waited. A short time later Dad and Steve pulled into the driveway. I stood up and got ready to go inside the house. Dad approached me and said, "You may as well sit back down, I called Kara and she said she would be about another hour." "Don't you have a key," I asked. "Kara has the only key to the house, we will just have to wait for her," Daddy replied. Looking bothered and trying to change the subject, Daddy continued, "Did you have fun skating?" I noticed Daddy's uncomfortable body language so I persisted in my questioning. "You mean to tell me, you don't have a key to your own home? What kind of man is not allowed a key to his own home?" I knew I had hit a bad cord with my daddy, and the tone of my voice was disrespectful but enough was enough, and I wanted some answers. With tears in his eyes Daddy simply replied, "I'm doing the best I can. I just want to keep this family together, and it is easier to let Kara have her way."

Feeling deep compassion toward our father, both Steve and I embraced him, and I apologized for my tone of voice and continued, "Tell us about our mother! I know Kara is not our mom, Steve and I talk about her a long time ago." Filled with lots of emotion while wiping the tears from his eyes, Daddy said, "Your mother and I loved each other very much. We got married, and a year later Steve was born. We were delighted to have a son but we didn't plan on having you so soon. Don't take that the wrong way, we loved having you, it was just really hard. We were both young and had to grow up really fast, especially your mother. I had to get a babysitter for you guys while I worked because you kids were too much for her to handle on her own. Kara was your babysitter.

"Your mother was pregnant with a baby by another man, and I got Kara pregnant with your little brother Bobby. Your mother and I divorced and Kara and I got married. I figured since she was a good babysitter, she would be a good mother for you and Steve. I've been trying to make this family work together ever since. It hasn't been all bad, has it?"

"It's not bad when you are home," I said, "but when you are gone, it's awful. Kara hates me, and I don't know why." I paused a moment then asked, "Dad, did you say, Mom had baby?" "Ya," Daddy continued, "you guys have a little sister, her name is Johanna. She is two weeks older than Bobby." I asked, "Can I meet her and my mother?"

"I'm sure you will when you get old enough," Daddy responded. Steve said out loud what I was thinking, "We are old enough now!" Daddy gave Steve a firm look, raised his voice and stated, "You guys are just going to have to wait, I already have to move this family around all the time because Kara don't want her finding you. Do you guys think I haven't talked to Kara about it? She won't even let me take you to see your mother, and Kara is going to really be pissed off, if she finds out I talk with you two about her."

Daddy said he loved all of us kids and didn't want to live without anyone of us. It was obvious to both Steve and me that our father was heartbroken. We knew our dad loved Bobby just as much as he loved us and I'm sure our father also loved Kara. As hard as it was for Steve and me to understand, and neither one of us wanted to admit it to ourselves, both of us knew, our father felt trapped and was completely lost in what to do about it. *Bobby, Steve, and I did not yet know God, but God knew us.*

2 Peter 2:19–21: "While they promise them liberty, they themselves are servants of corruption: for of whom a man is overcome, of the same is he brought in bondage. For if after they escaped the pollutions of the world through the knowledge of the Lord and Savior Jesus Christ, they are again entangled therein, and overcome, the latter end is worse with them than the beginning. For it had been better for them not to have known the way of righteousness, than, after they have known it, to turn from the holy commandment delivered unto them."

Because of the information provided to me by my birth mother about my father's spiritual life during their marriage, I believe my father was already saved and sealed unto salvation when this conversation took place. A person is a slave to whatever controls him. If we refuse to follow God, we will follow our own sinful desires and become enslaved to what our bodies want. When you have learned about Christ and have been positively influenced by other Christians, but then reject the truth and return to your sin, you are worse off than before, because you have rejected your only way out of sin. If we submit our lives to Christ, he will free us from the bondage to sin. *Christ frees us to serve him, resulting in our ultimate good.*

My daddy was like a man sinking in quicksand and had let go of the rope that had been given to him. Steve and I thanked Dad for telling us the truth concerning his union with Mom, promised him we wouldn't tell Kara of the conversation, and that we understood he was trying to do what he felt was best for us. Daddy seemed relieved and thankful for our submission to his authority. *Although Steve and I knew nothing about our heavenly Father, we both loved and respected our earthly father.*

Kara still had not returned home to let us in the house, so Steve grabbed the opportunity and changed the subject to something he had obviously been already talking to Dad about. Steve said, "Dad, I'm sixteen years old, I've been working with you every day since I was ten, and you know I work harder than anyone else. Will you please let me get my driver's license, get a car, and start paying me or let me get a job somewhere else so I can buy my own car." I also grasped hold of the opportunity to inform Daddy of a situation in my life. Although I was the one who prepared a healthy supper for the entire family most nights, I was not being allowed to eat it. Ever since my return home from the hospital where I had been treated for malnutrition, Kara had gone to the other extreme, and now I was receiving so much food on my plate there was no way humanly possible I could eat it all. Kara would make me sit at the table, looking at the plate of food until I heard the phone ring and her talking to Dad. Knowing her husband was about to return home she would then put the plate into the fridge and tell me "You will eat all this food even if it takes you all week." Kara never covered the plate so the air quickly dried out the food. She never warmed the leftover in the microwave, so the food was cold and hard. Sometimes it took as many as three days before I was able to choke down this nasty food. I then suggested to Daddy, "Why don't you just make a surprise visit home, and see for yourself."

To be locked out of our home, sitting on the porch with only Steve and Daddy for over an hour, and Kara and Bobby nowhere in sight, *I believe was a God given ordained moment in time, where the three of us could openly share our hearts with each other.*

Kara and Bobby returned from their shopping spree. The backseat and trunk were so loaded that some of the items had to be placed in the front seat between the two of them. Bobby jumped out, grabbed his food from Wendy's, ran to his bedroom and started playing on his Atari (video game of the time). Kara got out of the car, pointed at Steve and me and demanded, "You two get busy and unload this stuff." Kara grabbed the food she had gotten from Wendy's, went to kitchen table, sat down and started eating. Handing food to her husband, Kara said, "You go I watch TV and rest. You will have to work hard tomorrow in order to pay for all this stuff I bought." Dad took his food, flipped on TV, and sat down in his recliner. Steve and I carried everything inside the house and put it all away before we were allowed to eat. Kara had gotten a lot of groceries, and while she sat at the kitchen table eating she pointed and told Steve and me which cabinet to place each item. The last sack to be emptied had the ice cream in it, so Steve and I were called idiots because the ice cream had melted and we should have known better. By the time we had finished putting everything away, of course our food was already cold. Telling us to just be thankful for the food and to sit down and eat, Steve and I started to obey her. Just then Dad walked back into the kitchen. Dad put our food in the microwave, and gave it back to us warm to eat. Looking at Kara, Dad asked, "What else did you buy beside groceries?" Kara pulled out of the other bags, tons of new clothes for Bobby for school. Pointing at Steve and me, Dad questioned, "You didn't get anything for them?" Kara quickly responded, "Well yes of course I did, I got their school supplies also." Reaching into another bag, Kara brought out the required basic school supplies. Then handing a small handheld calculator to me (also required by the school for math class) she stated, "Your daughter better appreciate this, I search all over for it, and it cost a lot of money!"

I took the calculator from her, thanked her for it and thought to myself, math, yuk. Kara continued saying, "Maybe she won't be so stupid in math with that machine doing the work for her." I blurted out, "*I am not stupid*, I just don't get math! What about my other grades? You never say anything good about them! And I need this calculator because I have to learn algebra and the metric system! Do you know that stuff?" Kara glared at me and said, "Don't you talk that way to me in that tone of voice, young lady, you're getting to old for your britches." She then turned and faced Dad, saying, "See how she talks to me, she doesn't appreciate anything I do for her." Dad looked at me and said, "Cindy, finish eating, get your things and go to your room now!" Steve jumped up and slammed his fits down on the table trying to defend me, yelling at Dad, "It's about time Cindy started speaking up for herself, I can't believe you, Dad, taking Kara's side again, we're your kids, when are you going to stick up for us!"

Kara had started crying, Dad put his arm around her, and told Steve to go to his room also. Steve and I got up and obeyed our father.

Steve slammed his bedroom door so hard it shook the house, and as I walked down the hallway, Kara yelled, "And don't you think you will be going skating anymore this summer!" I closed my door, got into bed, and started crying. I thought to myself, "*I hate her!* I can't wait for school to start so I don't have to be around her and I can see my friends again. And, I finally stand up for myself, Daddy didn't protect me, and Kara took away my only joy of roller-skating." I fell asleep dreaming of the day when I would be free of her completely. My dream was always the same. I dreamed I was flying. The strange thing about this dream is that I was always flying upside down, backward, and doing the backstroke. Every morning as I sat on my bed, I would replay that dream in my head wondering what it meant. I thought to myself, "It must mean something, I keep having it over and over again." As I thought more on the matter, I imagined myself flying upward, strong and straight toward the stars, like super-girl or wonder-woman. I thought to myself, "Kara can take many things away from me, but she cannot take away my ability to dream!" Although *I did not yet know God, God did know me. His Spirit was giving me strength and courage through my dreams.*

About a week later, something amazing happened. Dad and Steve arrived home early. Dad had not called Kara to give her the heads up, so when he walked through the door, Kara was caught unaware. Kara run to the door and said, "What are you doing home so early, sweetheart? Why didn't you call me, so I could have had your supper ready for you?" Trying to put her arms around her husband, Dad pushed her aside, and came into the kitchen where I was sitting at the table with a plate of three-day-old, dried-up food in front of me. Daddy took one look at the plate of food and stated, "Cindy, put that in the trash, and, Kara, give my daughter some decent food to eat." In fear I looked at Kara, waiting to see what was going to happen next. Daddy saw the fear in my face and said, "Don't be afraid of her, you obey me and do as I say." I hurried up and did as I was told and with a fresh plate of food I sat down and started eating. "Where is Bobby?" Daddy asked me. I responded, "Bobby is at the next door neighbor's playing." Daddy replied, "Good," then turning his attention to Kara, he said in a surprising calm voice, "I'm sick and tired of you treating my daughter like she is some kind of slave and not feeding her properly. You make sure Bobby eats well!" Kara started crying and through her sobs tried to give Dad an explanation that would justify her actions. Kara said, "You told me to fed her well. Healthy and good foods. That is what I am doing. Now you're yelling at me for doing what you asked." Daddy responded, "Kara, it's not going to work this time, you may as well stop crying, I'm not falling for it anymore. I don't want to lose my child because you two can't get along with each other." Standing face to face with Daddy, Kara raised her voice and demanded, "Get rid of her then, do something with her and her brother Steve, I don't want either one of them around my son Bobby. They are a bad influence for him. Steve is disrespectful, and Cindy is unappreciative." Daddy asked, "What do you mean, Kara? The kids get along fine! It's not the kids, it's you!" Daddy looked my way, so I nodded my head up and down in agreement. Bobby, Steve, and I do get along with each other just fine. Daddy then told me to go to my room and pack up some of my clothes. He was going to take me to the lake house. Daddy packed the car with food and supplies and in my bag of clothes I packed a few books for reading. Kara insisted on coming along with Dad and me to the lake house, so Steve was left at home to take care of Bobby. The lake house was about an hour and half drive, and most of it was done in silence. When we got closer to our destination Daddy started talking, reassuring me he was not mad at me. He said he felt it would be better for everybody if there were some space between Kara and me. I told Daddy I agreed with him, thinking to myself, *"This is going to be great, no more Kara, I'm going to be free."*

Because Daddy worked long hard hours, it had been a long time since the family had visited the lake house. As we pulled up to the lake house, the first thing I noticed was how tall the weeds in the front yard were. So tall you could barely see the top of the double-wide trailer. Daddy went through the weeds first, just in case of snakes. There was a small front patio and once inside there was a strong musty smell. The trailer itself was furnished with nice cozy log cabin style fixtures. Size wise it was like a small two-bedroom house. Daddy checked out the water, lights etc., made sure the phone and TV worked, and put away the food he had brought for me. Daddy promised he would call me every morning before work and every night when he got home. Kara was busy looking around, trying to find work for me to do. "The lawn mower, wheelbarrow and shovels are in the shed. Clean up this place and dig up those rocks in the back yard. I expect at the very least one wheelbarrow full of rocks per day to be carried to the front yard and placed around the patio. Your dad's going to build me a rock wall out of them." I looked at Daddy and he nodded his head saying, "Do as your mom tells you to do." Kara smiled and said, "You didn't think you were going to be able to sit here and be lazy did you." Daddy smiled at me also and added, "It would help me out a lot. Make me proud of you, princess." With that said, Daddy kissed me on the forehead, and he and Kara left. "Yea," I screamed as soon as I saw the car disappear over the hill. *"I am free, free at last from the cruel, evil stepmother."*

I turned the radio on loud and started cleaning up the inside. I had a good time doing the work because I pretended it was my own house. I cooked myself sausage for supper and had pancakes covered with lots of syrup. I watched TV late and fell into a peaceful sleep listening to the crickets chirp. I got up early in the mornings before it got hot outside and did the work Kara required of me. Some other teenagers who were spending their summer vacation at their lake property saw me working in the yard, offered to help, and working together, the actual work time was only about one hour per day. With my new friends and their parents I went into town and they purchased for me a new swimsuit, and other age appropriate clothing for the lake. In the evening I was invited to spend time with them cooking hotdogs and marshmallows over an outdoor fire pit, and sometimes went out on the lake in their sailboat. This was a great family and with them I experienced what true love and respect for one another in a group unit was meant by God to be like. Daddy kept his promise and called me every night at 8:00 p.m. sharp and around 10:00 a.m. in the mornings. We would talk and laugh about the different things I had done during the day. I never told Daddy

ADOPTED BY THE KING

about the family I had met and was spending time with for three different reasons. First, I did not want to hurt Daddy's feelings for not being able to provide this type of home life for me. Second, I was afraid if Kara found out that I was having some good quality fun, she would make me come back home, and third, I did not want it to end. *I did not yet know of God, but God did know me. God knows that a child needs to be allowed to be a child, and a childhood should have good memories. The time spent with this amazing family was one of my good memories.*

Daddy was concerned about me being alone at night. I told him I slept on the couch while watching TV and that I was fine. Daddy told me he had a surprise for me and I would see it this next weekend. My surprise was my brother Steve and his friend Tom coming to visit. Steve was driving his own car! Steve told me Daddy really put Kara in her place, bought him this good enough until he can afford another car, and also rented for him and Tom a two-bedroom house for them to stay at. Daddy sent groceries and other supplies along with Steve and Tom. Included were three T-bone steaks for us to grill for supper that night. The guys had been given the instructions by Dad to enjoy the weekend at the lake, make sure the place is locked up tight and bring me back home because school was about to start.

Tom was eighteen and in my opinion, a semiattractive guy. He was very kind to me and that night he approached me sexually. This caught me off guard because I had never thought of myself in that way or that any guy might find me sexually attractive. I told Tom that I was not ready for sex to be a part of my life right now. He said he understood and he was willing to wait.

I was a freshman and looking forward to the first day at a high school level. Daddy had bought me some jeans and tops like all the other girls wore to school and had gotten me an after-school job at Sonic Drive In. School was released at 3:00 p.m. and I was to go straight from school to work. My job was a carhop and my hours were until 9:00 p.m. on the weekdays and some Saturdays. He bought me black pants and/or shorts to wear for work, and what was really cool was I could and was encouraged to wear my roller skates when I delivered the food to the customers. My boss was a friend

42

of Dad's and told me my dad had made arrangements with him for me to receive a half-hour break and food every night. I made lots of tips nightly and got a small paycheck weekly. Kara took all the money from me, telling me, "I'm keeping this for your college fund education."

When I needed some more personal hygiene products, I asked Daddy for money to purchase them. He said, "You have a job now, you can buy your own stuff." I then told him, "I have no money because your wife is taking it all from me." Daddy and Kara again had a very loud argument about money issues and things concerning me. Daddy bought me the items I needed, and told me from now on to keep all of my own earnings. I begged Daddy to please allow me to stay with Steve and Tom at their house. Daddy said, "You're a girl and you're only fifteen. What about your schooling?" I knew Steve had dropped out of school and was now working full time, so I promised Daddy, I would not do the same. With tears flowing down his cheeks, he said, "You're so young and beautiful. You have so much ahead of you, and you're not ready for what's out there. I did the best I could, and I'm sorry, I didn't make things easier for you." I reassured Daddy that I knew he had given it his all, that I would be safe with Steve, and that I would complete school. I laughed and said, "You're wife did teach me how to work and how to survive on my own." Then with a more serious tone I stated, "I can't stay in the same house with her for one more minute." Smiling at me Daddy said, "You are just like your mother, she is strong willed also." Daddy then agreed and allowed me to move in with my older brother. My little brother Bobby was only ten years old, still under the care of his mother, and unbeknown to me at the time, thirty-five years would pass before I would see Bobby again.

The next time I saw Bobby he was forty-five, married, and had four children. My husband had received information from a detective friend of ours that Daddy had been attending a church about a one-hour drive from our home. In hope that I would be able to reconnect with my daddy, we rode our motorcycles to this church every Sunday and stayed for all three services. On the forth try with no success, after the first service I approached the pastor, handing him a business card, and introduced myself saying, "I'm Don Johnson's daughter and this is my husband Jay. We've been attending this church for the past month in hope of seeing my father, but we are very active in our own church and need to return back, would you please place this business card into Don Johnson's hand and let him know I'm searching for him?"

The pastor looked puzzled and stated, "I've known Don and his son Bobby for years, I never knew he had a daughter." Smiling at the pastor, I replied, "That doesn't surprise me, very few people know I'm alive." The pastor then said, "Don is not here today, but that is his son Bobby right over there." Pointing first to Bobby, then with a movement of his hand, he pointed to a lady at the door and continued, "That's Bobby's wife, Ann over there." Jay took hold of my hand and started walking toward Bobby. As I headed in the same direction, I suddenly heard the Lord speak to my spirit saying, *"Go to Ann first, I know Ann and Ann knows me!"*

That's all I needed to hear. To know someone personally, you need to spend time with that person, and to know God shows spiritual maturity. (In God's eyes, Ann was such a person). Immediately I tugged on Jay's hand, changed the direction of my footsteps and headed toward Ann. When I reached her, I put my arms around her and introduced myself saying, "It is nice to meet you, my sister." She hugged me back, looked upon my face and questioned, "Do I know you?" I explained, "I am your husband's sister, Cindy." Seeing the confused look on her face, I continued slowly explaining, "Bobby— your husband—is my little brother. I am Cindy, Bobby's older sister and this is my husband Jay." Suddenly her facial expression changed from confusion to surprised, then she said, "Wait here, I will be right back." Ann then made a bee-line straight to Bobby. I watched her walk away, turn toward Jay and said, "Well, honey, I guess Bobby must have told her about me." Jay asked me why I went to Ann first. I simply stated, "God told me too. It will happen in God's way and in God's time. It has been thirty-five years since I last saw my brother, I can wait a few more minutes." At that time I saw Ann speaking to Bobby and pointing at me. "Now's the time," I said to Jay, taking him by the hand and walking toward Bobby. When I reached Bobby,

I threw my arms around him, got close to his ear and gently said, *"Remember, the people crucified Jesus, and he was an innocent man."*

Bobby hugged me back and asked, "How long have you been saved and why are you returning back now?" "I have been saved for a long time." I answered and continued saying, "I am returning back now because I asked God to give back to me all Satan has taken from me, and that includes a relationship between you and my father." The next church service was getting ready to start, so I asked Bobby if he minded if my husband and I sit with him and his wife. We stayed and after the service Jay and I went to lunch with Bobby, his wife, and children. Bobby's family are great people, his children were very respectful and allowed Bobby and I to talk without interruption. Bobby did most the talking and I listen very closely to all he said. He told me what he had been told about me. When he finished, I simply said, *"There are two sides to every story, the truth usually falls somewhere in the middle, and only when you know the whole truth are you able to walk in true freedom."*

John 8:31–38: "Then Jesus said to those Jews which believed on him, If ye continue in my word, are ye my disciples indeed; and ye shall know the truth, and the truth shall make you free. Then they answered him, We are Abraham's seed, and we were never in bondage to any man: how sayest thou, Ye shall be made free?

"Jesus answered them, Verily, verily, I say unto you, Whosoever commiteth sin is a servant to sin. And the servant abideth not in the house forever: but the Son abideth ever. If the Son therefore shall make you free, ye shall be free indeed. I know that ye are Abrahams's seed; but ye seek to kill me, because my word hath no place in you. I speak that which I have seen with my Father: and ye do that which ye have seen with your father."

Jesus made a distinction between heredity sons and true sons. The religious leaders were hereditary sons of Abraham (founder of the Jewish nation) and therefore claimed to be sons of God. But their actions showed them to be true sons of Satan, for they lived under Satan's guidance. Sin has a way of enslaving us, controlling us, dominating us, and dictating our actions.

Jesus is the only one who can break this power over your life.

Jesus himself is the truth that makes us free.

Jesus is the source of truth, the perfect standard of what is right.

Jesus frees us from the consequences of sin, from self-deception, and from deception by Satan.

Jesus shows us clearly the way to eternal life.

Your church membership and family connections will not make you a true son of God.

Your true father is the one you obey. Satan of lies or God of truth.

Jesus does not give us freedom to do what we want, but *freedom to follow God!*

As we seek to serve God, Jesus's perfect truth frees us to be *all that God meant us to be!*

By the conversation between my little brother and me, it was clear to me that although he was on the right path (thank you, Jesus), Bobby still needed to grow up in knowledge and understanding. Bobby believed what everybody else told him about me, instead of staying open to the possibility that he had been deceived by half-truths and downright lies. The same is true with our Lord and Savior, Jesus Christ. Instead of just believing what everybody else is telling you about Jesus, stay open to discovering the deeper truths for yourself.

Discovering knowledge and understanding while developing a personal relationship can only be done, by spending time with the person.

Experiencing False Freedom

Today with some knowledge of the Word of God, I believe it is safe to compare and describe the character of my father with a man found in the Bible. This man's name was Lot. Some people simply drift through life. Their choices, when they can muster the will to choose, tend to follow the path of least resistance. Lot was such a person. While still young, Lot lost his father. Although this must have been hard on him, he was not left without strong role models in his grandfather Terah and his uncle Abram, who raised him. Still, Lot did not develop their sense of purpose. When faced with decisions, he tended to put off deciding, then choose the easiest course of action. When given a choice, his first reaction was to think of himself. Lot, however, is called "just" and "righteous" (2 Peter 2:7, 8) and Lot was a successful businessman. Throughout his life he was so caught up in the present moment that he seemed incapable of seeing the consequences of his actions. Lot's life took an ugly turn and he blended so well into the sinful culture of his day, that he did not want to leave it. His drifting finally took him in a very specific direction—destruction. It is hard to imagine what his life would have been like without Abram's careful attention and God's intervention. God wants us to do more than drift through life; he wants us to be an influence for him.

Genesis 13:8–13: "And Abram said unto Lot, Let there be no strife, I pray thee, between me and thee, and between my herdmen and thy herdmen; for we are brethren. Is not the whole land before thee? separate thyself, I pray thee, from me: if thou wilt take the left hand, then I will go to the right; or if thou depart to the right hand, then I will go to the left. And Lot lifted up his eyes, and beheld all the plain of the Jordan, that it was well watered everywhere, before the Lord destroyed Sodom and Gomorrah, even as the garden of the Lord like the land of Egypt, as thou comest unto Zoar. Then Lot chose him all the plain of Jordan; and Lot journeyed east: and they separated themselves the one from the other. Abram dwelled in the land of Canaan, and Lot dwelled in the cities of the plain, and pitched his tent toward Sodom. But the men of Sodom were wicked and sinners before the Lord exceedingly."

Facing a potential conflict with his nephew Lot, Abram took the initiative in settling the dispute. Abram gave Lot his first choice, even though Abram had the right to choose first. Abram also showed a willingness to risk being cheated. Abram's example shows us how to respond to difficult family situations: (1) take the initiative in resolving conflicts, (2) let others have first choice, even if it means not getting what we want, (3) put family peace above personal desires.

The relationship between Daddy and me has many similarities to the relationship between Abram and Lot. Facing a potential conflict between his daughter and his wife, I took the initiative and encouraged Daddy to make a decision concerning my life. Daddy's decision to leave his fifteen-year-old daughter and his sixteen-year-old son completely on their own and return home to his wife and ten-year-old son was taking the path of least resistance. Daddy made the present wrong choice of abandonment of his two young children and seemed incapable of understanding the long-term consequence of his action. Steve and I certainly did not get what we wanted. We wanted our dad to be a part of our lives. Being separated from him and our little brother was very painful for us. Steve and I were freed of Kara's dominating authority but we had also lost the daily love and care of our father. Years before Steve and I were ready, we were forced to grow up, depend on each other for survival, and take responsibility for our own lives. Daddy's decision was a life-changing moment in our lives.

I lived with Steve and his friend Tom for the next two years. Together, we paid rent, utilities, and purchased our own food. I continued with the same school schedule and added later hours at Sonic. I also got another job at the Spagitti Spot on the weekends. During this time I also reconnected with my biological mother. She had grown into a beautiful woman with a delightful heart; I now understand why Daddy had continually told me that I look so much like my mother. All the physical attributes and the way we talk, walk, and stand are exactly the same. Mother had remarried and was at this time divorced. To my surprise I discovered I had two sisters and another brother. I'm no longer the middle kid; I'm now the eldest sister! At the time of this meeting, I was on Christmas break from school and I just turned seventeen. Johanna was twelve, Greg was eight, and my baby sister, Michelle, was six. At the time of divorce Greg and Michelle went with their father, so I only met my sister Johanna. Mother told me Michelle and Greg had a stepmother with behaviors similar to Kara, and she had lost contact with them also. As Mother provided many pictures of Steve and me during the first five years of our lives, so she provided several pictures of my sister Michelle and brother Greg. I promised her that I would not give up until I found all my siblings. It was ten years later when that amazing day happened and I met my little sister and brother for the first time.

Mother and I talked for several hours about her choices concerning Dad, my older brother, and myself. She kept a hope chest filled with items, pictures, and several pieces of legal documents proving that she did in fact try to make contact with Dad concerning Steve and me. Mother confessed she had made some bad choices in her life that affected the lives of her children, but she also took full responsibility for her choices, making no excuses, and never spoke anything negative about my father. I highly respected her honesty.

2 Corinthians 13:5–8 says, "Examine yourselves, whether you be in the faith. Prove your own selves, how that Jesus Christ is in you, except you be reprobates? But I trust that ye shall know that we are not reprobates. Now I pray to God that you do no evil; not that we should appear approved, but that you should do that which is honest, though we be as reprobates. For we can do nothing against the truth, but for the truth."

That you should do that which is honest, though we be as reprobates (fail the test) means our goal should not be merely to see others profess faith or begin attending church, but to see them become mature in their faith. Only then will we know if they are true Christians or imposters. As Christians, we should give ourselves spiritual checkups and see if we have a growing awareness of Christ's presence and power in our lives. We should be taking active steps to grow closer to God.

1 Corinthians 11:28: "But let a man examine himself, and so let him eat of that bread, and drink of that cup."

We are all sinners saved by grace. This is why we should examine ourselves through healthy introspection, confession of sin, and resolution of differences with others.

1 Corinthians 11:31: "For if we would judge ourselves, we should not be judged."

It was not my place to judge my mother, nor allow the choices she made in her younger days affect our time together in the future. Today I have a good solid relationship with my mother, and all my sisters and brothers on my mother's side of the family.

After spending some time with my mother I returned to Kansas City. When I got off the bus, police officers put me into handcuffs and arrested me. I asked what was happening and they explained that my parents told them I was a runaway. I told the officers this was not true and that I had been on my own for nearly two years. At the hands of the officers I endured a humiliating experience. I was made to be stripped of all my clothing and searched. I asked why this was happening to me, and informed that it was at the request of my mother. I informed the officers that woman was not my mother and did not have the right to insist on such a thing. I continued explaining to the officers, telling them the truth of why I choose to remove myself from under her authority over me. They then stated that as long as I was a minor child she did have authority over me and according to Missouri law that would remain until my seventeenth birthday. It was in that moment that God provided my way of escape. I told the officers that I had in fact turned seventeen years old one week earlier, on December 22 and I was born in 1962. I provided proof of this fact, received an apology from the officers, and informed that my stepmother had told them that I was only sixteen. Again, I informed the officers, I left home for that reason, to escape from her lies and authority over me.

2 Peter 2:9–13: "The Lord knoweth how to deliver the godly out of temptations, and reserve the unjust unto the day of judgment to be punished: but chiefly them that walk after the flesh in the lust of uncleanness, and despise government. Presumptuous are they, self-willed, they are not afraid to speak evil of dignities. Whereas angels, which are greater in power and might, bring not railing accusations against them before the Lord. But these, as natural brute beast, made to be taken and destroyed, speak evil of the things that they understand not; and shall utterly perish in their own corruption; And shall receive the reward of unrighteousness, as they that count it pleasure to riot in the day time."

God is able to rescue us from temptations and trials we face in a wicked world. Also, God will judge those who cause the temptations and trials, so we need never worry if justice will be done. The "dignities" are all the glories of the unseen world. Many people in our world today mock the supernatural. They deny the reality of the spiritual world and claim only what can be seen and felt. These people scoff at realities they do not understand, taking Satan's power lightly and thinking they have the ability to judge evil. Don't take Satan and his supernatural powers of evil lightly or feel arrogant about how defeated he will be. Although he will be destroyed completely, he is at work now trying to render Christians complacent and ineffective. People who do not believe these things to be true, are fools who will be proven wrong in the end.

To my surprise when I walked out the door of the police station, my daddy and his wife were waiting in their car. Motioning for me to get in the backseat, I obeyed, feeling safe, because my daddy was present. Kara was driving and I asked her to please drop me off at my brother Steve's house where I had been living at for the past two years. She started yelling and cursing at me saying, "How dare you, going to find your mother, after all I have done for you." She then drove to Twelfth Street (in Missouri, Twelfth Street was known for prostitution activity), told me to get out and find my own way back to Steve's. I begged Daddy not to allow her to do this to me, but with tears in his eyes, Daddy told me to get out. I obeyed, standing in the freezing cold, watching the car disappear from sight. I stood there a few minutes, expecting my daddy to convince his wife to turn around and come back for me. That never happened. Five years will pass before I will see Daddy again.

2 Peter 2:14–15: "Having eyes full of adultery, and cannot cease from sin; beguiling unstable souls: an heart they have exercised with covetous practices; cursed children: Which have forsaken the right way, and are gone astray, following the way of Balaam the son of Bosor, who loved the wages of unrighteousness."

Balaam was hired by a pagan king to curse Israel. He did what God told him for a while (Numbers 22–24), but eventually his evil motives and desires won out (Numbers 25:1–3; 31:16). Parents are to promote love and unity among the family. Kara viciously attacked my character and slandered my name because I disagreed with her opinions. Dad supported her evil words and deeds against me, which in my eyes and more importantly in the eyes of God made him just as guilty for those actions. If we refuse to follow God, we will follow our own sinful desires and become enslaved to what our bodies want. It was easier for Daddy to give in to Kara's demands than for him to protect the life of his daughter.

I did not have enough money for a cab, and thought to myself "How will I get home." At that moment an elderly couple pulled up, rolled down their window, and asked me if I needed help. I replied, "Yes, will you please take me to my brother Steve, about thirty miles from here?" This elderly couple drove me home, never asking any questions of what, why and how I arrived in the situation in which they found me. Sitting in the warmth of that backseat I welcomed the silence and reflected on my life thus far. I recalled the time I had spent under Kara's authority. At age five the emotional and psychological abuse started. Steve and I both had been told by Kara, that we would never amount to anything. Years of being exposed to degrading and belittling words breaks the spirit of a child! There were never any pictures of Steve and me taken and placed in the house. With no physical evidence of a child existence any child would feel as I did, unloved. Steve would cover my body as Kara would have fits of rage. Steve took many hard blows from Kara, was pushed down flights of stairs, and one time, while eating, Kara threw a fork at Steve so hard that it embedded into his forehead. Bobby was only ten years old when Steve and I left the house. All Bobby knew to be true was one day he had an older brother and sister and the next day he did not. Daddy had failed to protect Steve and me from the mental and psychological abuse of his wife. To survive those young years of my life, I trusted and relied on Steve to help me, and now in my teenage years I continued to relay on Steve for protection. The elderly couple broke my train of thought as we pulled in front of Steve's rental house saying, "Here you go, darling, is there anything else we can do for you?"

Matthew 25:34–40: "Then shall the King say unto them on his right hand, Come ye blessed of my Father, inherit the kingdom prepared for you from the foundation of the world: For I hungered, and you gave me meat: I was thirsty, and you gave me a drink: I was a stranger, and you took me in: Naked, and you clothed me: I was sick, and you visited me: I was in prison, and you came unto me. Then shall the righteous answer him, saying, Lord, when saw we thee and hungred, and feed thee? or thirsty, and gave thee drink? When saw we thee a stranger, and took thee in? or naked, and clothed thee? Or when saw we sick, or in prison, and came unto thee? And the King shall answer and say unto them, Verily I say unto you, Inasmuch as ye have done it unto one of the least of these my brethren, ye have done it unto me."

We have no excuse to neglect any person who has deep needs. I was deeply disappointed in my daddy for not taking responsibility for my safety and welfare, and allowing his wife to put his only daughter out on a street corner. Thank God, for this kindhearted couple who arrived at just the right moment and got me to a safe place. *I did not yet know God, but God did know me, and God discharges His angels to watch over me.*

I thanked the couple for their kindness and assured them that my brother and I would be just fine, after all I thought to myself, Steve and I have been taking care of each other for years. I ran inside and told Steve about all the events that had happened over the past week. I told Steve we have a wonderful mother who admitted to making some bad choices in her life, but had been praying for the return of her children. She had been repeatedly denied by Kara any visitation and was never allowed to speak to Daddy concerning us. Mom told me in time she lost hope of ever seeing us again.

It was with Tom that I began my search for love. I entered into a sexual relationship with him. At that time Tom was nineteen years old, very kind, and attractive. It felt appropriate and right, however, my feelings were all over the place. I did not understand these emotions I was experiencing. Both Tom and I were very immature. I was not using any form of birth control, neither Tom or I wanted an unplanned child, so Thank God we did have the common sense to use condoms. Engaging in sex outside of marriage is not God's plan for his children. *I did not yet know God, but God did know me and God's hedge of protection was all around me.*

I was a senior and education had always been very important to me. I returned to Grandview Sr. High where I had been attending previous years. I was called into the office and told I could no longer attend. I asked why. I had always been a good student and carried good grades. I was told that my mother had called to inform them that I no longer lived at their home, and since I was no longer in the school district I could not attend school. I enrolled at Ruskin Heights, the high school in the district in which I did live. I attended every class daily, maintain good grades, and worked two jobs; I was tired but doing okay. About two months passed and again I was called to the office and told I could no longer attend high school. I asked why. I was told Kara had informed the school that my parents did not live in the Ruskin Heights district therefore they were paying school taxes for another school district and unless I paid tuition, which was much more than I could afford, they had no other option but to enforce the legal requirements. I was *heartbroken.*

Colossians 3:21, 25: "Fathers, provoke not your children to anger, least they be discouraged. But he that doeth wrong shall receive for the wrong which he hath done: and there be no respect of persons."

Kara found the legal loophole and stole away my privilege of graduation. Why, I asked myself, was this woman pursuing me with her evil ways. In my opinion, the answer is, she would do whatever it takes to make sure I would not succeed in life.

Christ transcends all divisions between people and the Word of God says Christians are to work hard and be fair.

I did not give up. I paid a fee, took the GED test, passed the test the first time with flying colors, and started pursuing the desire of my heart. I started looking into cosmetology school.

Hebrews 13:6: "So that we may boldly say. The Lord is my helper, I will not fear what man shall do unto me."

We become content when we realize God's sufficiency for our needs.

I returned home early one day and discovered Tom having sex with another woman. I was devastated. During that same week, my brother Steve announced that in six months he would be joining the marines. I needed to find a new place to live and a better job to support myself. I wanted to get as far away from Kara as possible to avoid her interfering in my life. I acquired a fake ID, stating I was twenty-four, saved money, and was able to rent a small-furnished apartment located near downtown Kansas. I also found two waitress jobs. The first was at a coffee shop from 6:00 a.m. to 1:00 p.m., and the second was a truck stop from 3:00 p.m. to 10:00 p.m. I didn't mind the long hours, the atmosphere was pleasant, and the tips were great. I worked hard and was very responsible with my earnings. Paying rent and bills and purchasing for myself, professional-style type of clothing. I had begun to develop physically and was quickly becoming a beautiful young woman. I was looking and acting as if though I were in fact twenty-four years old. Things went well for about six months.

I made the decision to search for a different type of job, and took a couple of days off work to pursue this desire. I got up early in the morning, dressed in the most professional outfit I could put together, and waited for the bus to take me downtown. While I waited a taxi pulled up, the driver asked me where I was going and if I needed a ride. I explained I was headed downtown to submit job applications and only had enough money for the bus. The driver said he was headed in that direction, and would drop me off. No charge. I accepted the offer, arrived downtown, submitted many applications, and returned to the bus stop for a ride back home. Several hours had passed, and it was starting to get dark. As I waited for the bus, to my surprise the same cab driver reappeared and offered me a ride home. Again at no charge. I thanked him, hopped into the cab, and gave him my home address. While sitting at a stop sign, I noticed a man approaching the cab. He was wearing a turtleneck shirt and pulling the collar up over his face. I screamed at the driver to get out of here, just as I felt the end of a gun against my forehead. The robber reached in the cab and grabbed my purse, which was placed in the seat next to me. I was frozen in fear. As the robber ran away, the cab driver reached into his glove box, pulled out a gun, and fired shots into the air. As frightened as I was, I did know that I had been set up. I got out of the cab, called the driver a few choice words and told him I would walk the rest of the way home. I ran all the way. Still shaken I managed to get the keys into the lock, turn the knob, and get into my apartment. I did not have a phone, so I could not call for help. I then heard a knock at the door. Looking through the peephole, I saw it was the cab driver and another man.

I remembered I had given him my address. I remained silent, hoping they would leave. After a few moments of trying to convince me that he was just concerned for my safety, they broke my door down and overpowered me. They stuck a needle into my arm and I went unconscious. When I awoke I was in a strange room, lying on a bed, undressed, and handcuffed to the floor heater. I started screaming, the two men appeared, restrained me, and drugged me again. Several men were raping me repeatedly. Many hours passed, and at times I would wake up, looking around the room, trying to find a way of escape. I was bleeding uncontrollably, and I was very weak. I drifted in and out of consciousness. I had no sense of time, or how many days had passed. Food was placed on the floor next to the bed and I did eat the food and drink the water. I began to get a little strength back. I started screaming and hitting the floor heater with my hands when I heard a key turning in the lock.

A lady appeared, looking at me with a face full of hurt, pain, and confusion. She unlocked the handcuffs, washed away the blood, helped me get dressed, and was talking very fast. She told me she was helping me to get away because she had heard the men talking about what they were going to do with me. One of the men was her husband and father of her two children. She would take me to someone who could help me, but begged me not to tell anyone, for she feared for her life and the lives of her children. Just wanting to escape from this situation with my own life: I agreed not to tell. I asked how long I had been here. She told me that to the best of her I knowledge it had been several days, maybe a week. She took me to a clubhouse, talked with an older man, and left. *I did not yet know God, but God did know me, and God chose me, even before I knew of Him.*

Psalms 124:8: "Our help is in the name of the Lord, who made heaven and earth."

Do you ever feel trapped by overwhelming odds? With God there is always a way out because he is the Creator of all that exists. No problem is beyond his ability to solve; no circumstance is too difficult for him. We can turn to the Creator for help in our time of need, for he is on our side. God will provide a way out.

Hebrews 4:16: "Let us therefore come boldly unto the throne of grace, that we may obtain mercy and find grace to help in time of need."

Prayer is our approach to God, and we are to come "boldly unto the throne of grace." Some Christians approach God meekly with heads hung, afraid to ask him to meet their needs. Others pray flippantly with little thought. In my confused and lost mind, I cried out for help, I cried out for my brother Steve to find and rescue me. Today, I know that God heard my cry for help and that he understood and was not offended at my lack of knowledge in him. Today, I also know that we are to come before the throne of grace with reverence and with bold assurance, for he is our King, our friend, and counselor.

At the time of the kidnapping and rape, I had no knowledge or understanding of the hidden evil that surrounded the circumstances of the rape. As my life unfolded, many more unexplainable things continued to happen, and in time when I made the decision to give control of my life to God, the painful truth of this situation was revealed to me. As you continue to journey with me through my life, I will answer the questions of how, when, and who. Please continue reading.

A man came over and introduced himself as Jim. He was the owner of the club. He offered me food and said he would help me. I believe I was still in shock from the ordeal, and I still was dizzy from all the drugs in my system. I began to talk, telling him what had happened to me. I told him I was seventeen, I could not return home because the kidnappers knew where I lived and I feared for my life.

Jim told me he is a single father to a seven-year-old daughter and that I could stay with him while I healed. He also said that I should not report the kidnapping and rape because the police would say I brought the situation upon myself due to my own behavior and bad choices. He also reminded me of the woman who had placed her own life in jeopardy for helping me. I believed this man, and the kidnapping and rape went unreported. Jim went with me to my apartment so I could collect my belongings, and close out my agreement with the landlord. I contacted both of my waitress jobs, and discovered I no longer had either job. Being both homeless and jobless, I accepted Jim's offer to stay at his home in exchange for caring for his child while my body healed. Jim was very kind to me and his daughter was a great kid. I was given my own room. I cleaned his house and watched his child when she returned home from school in the afternoon. I cooked dinner every night and often left food in the microwave for Jim to eat when he returned home from work. I got my driver's license and Jim purchased me a small car. A couple of months had passed and my bruises had faded. My body seemed to be healing well, however I was gaining quite abet of weight, and I had not had a monthly cycle. I made a doctor appointment and found out I was two months pregnant with possible twins. Jim provided me the money for an abortion. I was full of confusion and shame. The emotional pain for what I had done was overwhelming me so I turned to Jim for comfort, and entered into a sexual relationship with him.

Jim was fifty-four years old and I was about to turn eighteen. Jim was twice divorced and had fathered ten children by four different women. After a few weeks I also became pregnant again. I got a job at Jim's clubhouse as a cocktail waitress, serving mixed alcoholic drinks to the customers. Jim's clubhouse was a well-known gentlemen club, with a large stage where female dancers performed daily for the male costumers. Behind the counter there was a door that led upstairs where there were four rooms furnished with beds, used by the dancers and clients for paid sexual exchanges. The club was licensed for age twenty-one and above, however since I had a fake ID and I knew the owner, Jim encouraged me to work there. I started in the club as a cocktail waitress, but quickly escalated to a dancer, and in time I also partook in paid sexual services with the clients. Jim's charge for the use of the upstairs rooms was ten dollars per every fifteen minutes. I was young, attractive, and new on the scene. I preformed sexual acts with an average of five to ten clients per day. Jim made a large amount of money daily from the fee he charged for the use of the room. At that time Jim never asked for any of the money I pocketed for the sexual services. Without giving it much thought at the time, I had become a stripper and a prostitute.

My physical body was very weak and I lost the unborn child to stillbirth during the sixth month. The doctors told me that due to the stress and abuse of my body I might never be able to conceive a child. I returned back to work as soon as I was able. As ridiculous as this sounds, I enjoyed being part of this lifestyle. The daytime atmosphere of the club life was pleasant. I worked 9:00 a.m. to 3:00 p.m. and watched Jim's child after school. Most of the customers at the club were older professional businessmen and the money and tips were great. I charged whatever amount I felt appropriate for the sexual service requested. Being allowed to make my own decisions, without any interference about my life, felt good. At age eighteen

I traded the old car Jim had bought me and paid cash for a new car. I enrolled myself in cosmetology school, paid the initial down payment, was informed of the start date, what is expected of me concerning class times and attendance, and what the monthly tuition would be. Prostitution was not my profession of choice, I wanted to be a hair designer. I truly felt like I was in control of my own life for the first time.

School was from 9:00 a.m. to 5:00 p.m., Monday thru Friday. Jim made other arrangements for after school care for his daughter, so I worked at the club from 7:00 p.m. to 2:00 a.m. and all day on Saturday. There was a great change in the atmosphere of the club during these hours. Filled with high levels of alcohol the behaviors of the customers were rude, distasteful and unruly. There was a large amount of illegal drugs going through the club. I never partook in the drug scene and I never drank alcohol while at the club. I wanted to be in full awareness of all that took place around me at all times. After the rape, I no longer trusted anyone. I chose to stay in the night environment because of the greater increase of tips for dancing.

One night after I had completed a stage dance I sat down at one of the back tables and started studying for a major test I would be taking the next day at school. A middle-aged man sat down at the table and asked me many questions. "What are you studying, why are you here, how old are you?" I answered, "Got a test I got to pass tomorrow, paying my way through school, why is my age your concern?" More questions came my way, this time about the cost for sexual favors. "Not interested," I told the man. "Come on," he said, "don't want to make your pimp mad atcha, do you?" "Nobody controls my life, but me!" I replied. "These other girls may give their money to a pimp, I don't, I'm only here until I finish school, then I'm out of here." He offered me drugs and alcohol. I told him "I don't use." Just then the club was raided by police. I looked at the man as he flashed his badge at me. "SHIT!" I blurted out. "I gotta take this test and pass it tomorrow, the next opportunity for this test is not for six months!"

The officer looked at me with compassion in his eyes and asked questions, "I have a daughter your age, where are your parents?"

"Don't want me," I replied. "If I let you walk out of here will you promise not to come back?" I responded, "I appreciate you letting me walk, I don't have a record and I don't want one. As far as that promise you are asking me to make, I have a question for you, will you pay my school tuition?" He shook his head slowly back and forth, no. "I didn't think so," I said, "and I cannot make that promise to you." The sergeant approached the officer, "What about this one?" he asked. The officer responded, "She's clean, let her go." All the girls working that night were arrested for drug use. Jim received several citations. Although I could have been arrested for being under age and solicitation, the officer believed me, and allowed me to walk free that night. I still have a clean record, and thirty years later, this officer and I crossed paths again. Today he is one of my customers at the barbershop my husband and I own together. *I did not yet know God, but God did know me. God knew ahead of time, His plan for my life.*

Mark 1:40–41: "And there came a leper to him, beseeching him, and kneeling down to him, and saying unto him, If thou wilt, thou can make me clean. And Jesus, moved with compassion, put forth his hand, and touched him, and saith unto him, I will; be thou clean."

Although a person's body may be full of disease, the person inside is no less valuable to God. We have all been diseased by the ugliness of sin. But God, by sending his Son Jesus, has touched us, giving us the opportunity to be healed.

In 1981 at age nineteen, I graduated cosmetology school and received my class *A* license. The type of license I hold is important because there are many different levels of cosmetology. This license required the maximum number hours available to be completed, opening up opportunities in a variety of options in the field of cosmetology. I had also saved enough money to move on in my personal life.

Up to this point, Jim had supported all the decisions I made concerning my life. Jim had encouraged the advancement in education, cooperated with me in the necessity of the rearrangements concerning his child, and he had never requested any financial means for providing me shelter and food. The sexual relationship between us was consensual. I informed Jim of my intent to move into my own apartment and at that time he requested financial payback for all he had done for me during the past couple of years. Feeling obligated I submitted all of my savings to him, thinking I could replace it all in less than six months. I was ready to move forward, get a job in cosmetology, and put this life of prostitution behind me. Jim's behaviors changed dramatically. I very quickly became his piece of property. Jim watched every move I made, he chose the clothes I was to wear and the amount of makeup I was to apply. Jim sold my car, saying he would take and pick me up from any place I needed to go. I no longer was allowed to have my own bedroom, and sex with him, was upon his demand. Jim brought men and women to the house, and for a fee set by him, I was commanded to perform sexual acts with them. Many times Jim would just watch the sex act, sometimes he would engage in the sex act. I was humiliated, and beaten down verbally during the performance. If I displayed any form of sexual pleasure I was beaten physically.

One time after a sex act with a couple, the lady and I went into the bathroom to clean up. Leaving the faucet running to cover the conversation, I asked her to please help me. She said her husband and she were told by Jim that this was what I wanted. We were interrupted by a knock on the bathroom door and Jim's voice asking what was taking us so long. The couple left and about one hour later the phone rang. After Jim finished the conversation with the caller, he beat me more severely than ever before, knocking out my front teeth.

A few days later I tried to commit suicide. I took a large amount of pain pills with a large amount of alcohol. I passed out and the next thing I remember was waking up in a cold shower. Jim had found me on the bathroom floor, put me in the shower, and revived me. Jim told me if I ever tried to leave him again, he would kill me himself. I hated my life and I hated this man who treated me like a piece of property. I knew if I was to survive this evil that I could no longer resist. Jim was much stronger than me. I submitted to his authority over my life, waiting for a day when I could escape. I was now forced to work at his club. Due to the attention I received from the male customers, Jim was filled with jealousy and rage and so possessive of me, that he chose for me what clients I could and could not perform sex acts with. Jim took all the money I received from the clients. For about six months I was physically, mentally, emotionally abused and sexually assaulted numerous times.

Proverbs 6:25–35: "Lust not after her beauty in thane heart: neither let her take thee with her eyelids. For by means of a whorish woman a man is brought to a piece of bread: and the adulteress will hunt for the precious life. Can a man take fire in his bosom, and his clothes not be burned? Can one go upon hot coals, and his feet not be burned? So he that goeth in to his neighbor's wife; whosoever touched her shall not be innocent. Men do not despise a thief, if he I steal to satisfy his soul when he is hungry; but if he be found, he shall restore sevenfold; he shall give all the substance of his house, but whoso committed adultery with a woman lacketh understanding: he doeth it destroyed his own soul. A wound and dishonor shall he get; and his reproach shall not be wiped away. For Jealousy is the rage of a man: therefore he will not spare is the day of vengeance. He will not regard any ransom; neither will he rest content, though thou give many gifts."

Although this passage is directed toward men, women should heed this wise advice as well. Some people argue that it is all right to break God's law against sexual sin if nobody gets hurt. In truth, somebody always gets hurt. People are devastated. Children are scared. The partners themselves, even if they escape disease and unwanted pregnancy, lose their ability to fulfill commitments, to feel sexual desire, to trust, and to be entirely open with another person. God's laws are not arbitrary. The law does not forbid good, clean fun; rather, the law warns us against destroying ourselves through unwise actions or running ahead of God's timetable. A person who has no purpose in life is simpleminded. Without aim or direction an empty life is unstable and vulnerable to many temptations.

When I was a child, I had learned how to get what I wanted by telling Kara the exact opposite of what I truly wanted. For example, at Thanksgiving dinner, I would request the white meat from the turkey, tell her how much I hated dark meat, and always without fail, I would receive just what I truly wanted, which was dark meat. Kara, unknowing, had actually taught me strong survival skills against evil. *I did not yet know God, but God did know me. God knew I needed to be taught how to live a life pleasing to Him.*

I used these skills with Jim. In time, he allowed me to drive myself to and from the club. I chose my own clothes, and was allowed to spend some money on myself. He no longer seemed concern about my makeup (I don't like to wear large amounts). Jim still controlled my sex life, but the physical and verbal abuse became much less often. It had been approximately one year since that sever beating I received at the hands of Jim and my submission to his control over my life, when I received a phone call from my brother Steve. Steve had returned home from the marines, had married a lady named Judy, and needed a place to stay until they could financially afford to purchase their own home. I requested, and was granted permission from Jim, to allow my brother and his wife to stay in the basement of Jim's house. They moved in and made the basement into a nice apartment. Judy became pregnant and gave birth to a beautiful baby girl named Ashley. They stayed in the house for a total of about one year then moved into their own home. During that year, I continued to go daily to Jim's club performing sexual exchanges with male clients.

Judy and I became very close and we talked often. Some people may ask, why, did I not tell her about the bondage and captivity I was in. The answer is, I was filled with shame. I was broken, beaten down, had lost all self-respect and hope of ever escaping. I did not want her or my brother to know the truth. The shame in me was overwhelmingly strong. I simply savored the moments I spent with her, my brother, and my newborn niece. In their presence, life for me, seemed somewhat normal, and I did not want to do or say anything that might disrupt it. After they moved, I stayed in touch with Steve, Judy, and Ashley.

Steve became physically and verbally abusive to his wife and daughter. Together, Judy and I committed Steve into a mental illness facility where he was diagnosed with disorganized schizophrenic behaviors. Because of Steve's uncontrollable fits of rage, we made the very painful decision of placing him into a state institute in hope that under their care Steve would in time be healed, Kara (mine and

Steve's stepmother) told Judy to divorce her husband. I encouraged Judy to make a decision based on what was best for her and her daughter. In time Judy was persuaded and convinced divorce was her only option if she was to provide a safe environment for their child Ashley. It takes supernatural strength and courage to make a positive decision for your life and the life of an innocent child, when you have no understanding of why it needed to be made in the first place. I thank God for his love toward this family unit. I continued to stay involved in my brother's progress concerning his mental illness. In time the doctors working with Steve found the right medicine to control his negative behaviors. Steve gets a monthly injection of this medicine and has become what I describe as a gentle giant, now only experiencing anger outburst, when someone or something disrupts his routine.

At the time of this writing, thirty years later, Judy has not remarried. As a single mother to Ashley, Judy worked two jobs to support their child, and just informed me, that at age sixteen Ashley received a large check from the state for back child support on behalf of her daddy. In life, things often change as time goes on. In our lives this one true fact remained the same, Judy loved her husband, Ashley loves her daddy, and I love my brother.

Steve has recently received a full grant awarded by the Veterans of America, and remains under their care. My husband and I visit with my brother weekly, taking the gospel message to Steve and the other veterans. One day the message was about how to live out your life in the resurrection power of our living Lord and Savior. After the message, Steve approached me and stated, *"Sis, I want this power to live inside of me."* My husband, and some other men helped Steve to fully understand his decision.

With God's power now living in him, my brother submitted and willing went through detox from his addiction to alcohol. At the time of this writing, Steve still struggles with his addiction, stumbling and falling from time to time. In God's perfect timing I believe my brother will be completely set free of his addiction. For now I am content with my brother progress. Steve has received a fighting spirit from God, for when he stumbles, Steve always gets back up, shakes it off, and continues moving forward. Judy has extended full forgiveness unto Steve (knowing that what Steve is experiencing is by no fault of his own) and Ashley accepted and continues to love her mentally ill daddy. By God's amazing mercy, grace, and love, God extended his mighty hand down from the heavens, built bridges over troubled waters, and reconciled separated lives. *This time, I say, my brother who did not know God, does today.*

At age twenty-one, I again became pregnant, but not with an unwanted child. I did want to give life to this unplanned, unexpected miracle growing inside of me. I chose not to tell anyone of the pregnancy (especially Jim) and was able to conceal the identity of this child well into my seventh month. Knowing I would soon be responsible for the life of my child, I mustard up the courage to ask Jim's permission to look for a job in the area of cosmetology. With this license I received a job working at a spa, doing nails and make-up. I requested and received specific work hours at the spa, therefore making it impossible for me to continue working nights at Jim's clubhouse. This change allowed me to get the rest needed to carry a healthy child.

In time the weight gain and visibility of the pregnancy became known to Jim. Not wanting to father another child and discovering that I had purposely withheld the information from him, Jim became very angry. Over the remainder of the pregnancy, things were very difficult for me. Abortion was no option so Jim tried to convince me to give the child up for adoption. I flatly refused, but the stress, anxiety, and confusion began to overwhelm me. I found a doctor and began prenatal care. In July 1984 I gave birth to my child. She is healthy and beautiful. I was a young twenty-two-year-old mother with no clue about what to do next. I remembered seeing a movie where after the birth of his child, the father lifted up his daughter, asking for a blessing from God upon her. I had always believed in a power greater then myself and as the doctors placed my daughter into my arms, again I cried out for help! Looking up I said, "Thank you for this child! Give to me the ability to love her unconditionally!" Not knowing or understanding what I had just done, I do believe that in that moment I received from God the ability to love people unconditionally. *I did not yet know God, but God did know me, and my child.*

Psalms 103:13–14: "Like as a father pitieth his children, so he pitieth them that fear him. For he knoweth our frame; he remembereth that we are dust."

We are fragile, but God's care is eternal. Too often we focus on God as judge and lawgiver, ignoring his compassion and concern for us. When God examines our lives, he remembers our human condition. Our weakness should never be used as justification for sin but His mercy takes everything into account. Trust him. God will deal with you compassionately.

Jim arrived at the hospital that day accompanied with a lady from the adoption agency. She seemed surprised that I had no intention of giving up my child for adoption. She explained to me that both mother and father of the child had legal rights in this decision, and seeing that I was determined to keep my child, she left. I named my daughter Renee. Having nowhere else I to go I returned back to Jim's house with our child in my arms. Not trusting anyone else to care for Renee I quit my job at the spa and got a job at an area child-care facility from 6:00 a.m. to 6:00 p.m. The owner allowed Renee into the nursery while I worked. Renee needed many baby items so Jim allowed me to keep my paychecks. Renee always got what she needed, but I often purchased secondhand items in order to save half the pay. I opened up a savings account, waiting for an opportunity for Renee and me to leave. The environment at the house changed dramatically. There was calmness and a sense of joy that I had never felt there before. In a few short weeks, Jim began to hold and interact with Renee. It was obvious that he loved her. Jim and I learned to cohabitat together for the sake of our daughter. We gave each other plenty of personal space and the physical and verbal abuse ceased, *I did not yet know God, but God did know me. God knew I needed to learn how to bring up a child in Him.*

When Renee was about eighteen months old, I decided to go through the items she no longer needed and had a small yard sale. A neighbor I had never met before arrived at the sale carrying her own child in her arms. As the children played, this lady and I started a conversation.

This lady asked, *"Do you believe in God?"* "Yes," I responded, "I do believe in something greater than myself, I guess that would be God." Smiling gently, she focused all her attention on me and looking straight into my eyes, she then asked the most important question I had ever been asked, *"Do you know His Son, Jesus?"* To this question I replied, *"Never heard of the man, who is he?"* Placing her hand into mine she said, "Come with me to church and Bible study and I will I introduce him to you." I did go, I listened, and believed what I heard about all this wonderful Son of God had done for me thousands of years ago at Calvary. I had managed to save enough money and one day after church I told Jim that Renee and I would be moving out. Jim told me that I was free to go but I could not take Renee. Jim threatened me with my past, saying he would tell everyone, including my church friends about my life of being a prostitute. He convinced me that the law would grant him sole custody of our daughter and I would not be allowed to see her again. Jim gave me the ultimatum that if I wanted to continue to stay at his house with our daughter, I must marry him.

I did not want anyone to know about my past, and I was very naive about the law concerning the legal rights of Renee and myself. The one thing I was certain of is—that I would rather spend my lifetime in bondage with my daughter, than to spend one moment in freedom without her. I agreed to marry Jim to not be separated from Renee. That day was an awful event in my life, my stomach was upset and I spent much of the day vomiting. That day was never remembered or celebrated. I thought that Jim and I would continue coexisting together in the same living arrangements prior to the marriage. That was not true. Jim forced himself upon me and told me that it is a wife duty to be sexually submissive to her husband and I was to obey him.

During the week I continued to work at the childcare facility and go to church on Sunday. Many times Jim would attend church with Renee and I. The people at church were very kind and I became friends with many of them. I joined a Wednesday night Bible study and often went to the movies or out to dinner with the other women. I often wondered why nobody questioned my relationship with Jim. I was a beautiful woman in my early twenties, and Jim was a plain looking man in his early sixties.

During this time frame, I also tried reconnecting with my dad. As in the past, I had to request Kara's permission first. I made the phone call and of course, as always, Kara answered. I said, "I now have a daughter, and would like for Renee to have active grandparents in her life." I had to promise Kara not to speak of my brother Steve, or my mother Ellen. I was also informed that I was to call her Mom. I agreed with all the conditions and Kara agreed to give it a try and gave me their new address. When I arrived at their new home, it was obvious that Daddy's heating and cooling business must be successful. Their very large home was absolutely gorgeous. I introduced Renee and Jim to my parents. Dad was overjoyed at my return and loved his grandchild. Although Jim was ten years older than he, Dad and Jim seem to really like each other. Jim told Dad how much he loved me and how he planned to take care of me forever. For me, it was appalling. How could my father even begin to think I was happy? Was he completely blind? After a few more visits, I had a much better understanding of the situation. Kara was always screaming about ridiculous things and belittling Daddy in front of his employees. Everything to be done and every decision to be made was to be done upon her command and the way she wanted it, no exceptions, ever! Through it all, my father would smile, laugh, and joke about his wife's behaviors. I can only recall three good things that I saw in that house during the short time frame of my return. First, I got to spend some time with my childhood protector, Uncle Dale, and he got to meet my daughter. Second, my little brother, Bobby, was away at college, and third, Judy often brought Ashley, Steve's daughter over for the day while she worked. I knew I would never trust Kara alone with Renee because of what I had experienced as a child in her care, and what I saw and heard on my last day in her presence reassured me of that fact.

Ashley was one year older than Renee and had just starting potty training. Ashley had a bowel movement accident in her underwear. Kara took the dirty underwear, smeared the bowel movement onto Ashley's face saying, "You will not ever make a mess like this again while you are with me." She then made Ashley wash out her own panties in the stool before she was allowed to wash off her face.

I tried to intercede for Ashley, but was told I would never be a good mother because I was too soft. Kara said, "If you want to be a good mother, you need to put fear into a child while they are still young, otherwise, they will walk all over you, when they get older." In that moment, I remembered all my own fear that I felt toward Kara. In that moment, I just wanted to get as far away from Kara as possible and rescue my own daughter, preventing any future experiences she may have to endure at the hands of Kara. As I gathered up our things, preparing to leave, Kara asked, "Are you and your family coming over for Thanksgiving dinner next week? If you do, I would like for you guys to park behind the house and come in through the back door, because I don't want the neighbors to see Renee and think bad about this family." I looked at my beautiful olive-skin-toned daughter, and replied, "I'm sure we will have other plans for Thanksgiving." *I did not yet know God, but God did know me. God knew it was time for me to take responsibility and grow up.*

As I was driving down the street, I saw Daddy's work van coming around the corner. I motioned for him to pull over and told him, "I will not be coming back here again. I cannot be around your wife anymore and I will not allow my daughter around her." As I have seen in the past, Daddy started wiping tears from his eyes, and said, "I can't divorce her, everything is in her name, she will take everything I've worked so hard for." I felt deep compassion for my dad and stated, "I'm not asking you to divorce your wife. *I'm asking you to be a part of my life and your granddaughter's life.* Is all that (pointing toward his house) more important to you, than us?" My daddy just stood there with his face looking at the ground. He did not say another word. His silence, his unspoken words, said everything I did not want to hear. With tears now in my eyes, I said, "I love you, Daddy, have a good life."

I was leaving my daddy that day as a scared and lost little child. Twenty-five years of time would pass before I would see him again.

When I returned back into the life of my daddy, I will be a mature, confident, courageous woman of God.

I rolled up the window and drove back to my house. I say my house, because I was returning to a place where there was no love between the father of my child and me. This place did not feel like a home to me. I remembered the dream I repeatedly had as a child. Flying upside down and backward. *If I could just fly far away from it all, I thought to myself.* My thoughts changed as a stark reality hit me hard. My behaviors and choices in life were very much like Daddy's! I also had allowed people to control my life. From the outside, everything appeared to be good between Jim and me. I had never told anyone what was really happening to me. I was full of guilt and shame. That day *I made a firm decision* in my mind, if I was to find happiness in my life, *I would have to be the one to make some changes, starting with myself.*

1 Corinthians 14:11–12: "When I was a child, I spake as a child, I understood as a child, I thought as a child: but when I became a man, I put away childish things. For now we see through a glass, darkly; but then face to face: now I know in part; but then shall I know even as also I am known."

This verse offered a glimpse into the future to give us hope that one day we will be complete when we see God face-to-face. We don't have all the answers now, but then we will. Someday *we will see Christ in person and be able to see with God's perspective. This truth should strengthen our faith.*

Seeking True Freedom

I had a dream that night and would periodically have this dream over the next twenty-five years. I was sitting at a table looking at a jigsaw puzzle. The container that held the puzzle pieces was nowhere in sight, so I had no idea what the incomplete picture was to be like. All the pieces were turned upside down and scattered all around. I started finding all the straight edge pieces, turning them over and began working on the border. At times I would try jamming the pieces together, forcing them to fit. Of course, this never worked. I would then lay the piece aside for a while, go back later, and try again. Although the puzzle continued to develop, I was unable to see the finished product. The day I turned over the last piece, I placed it in the center of the puzzle, and suddenly the completed picture took form. The last piece fit snugly into the heart of an eagle, soaring high over mountains. That day was also the day that I reconnected with my physical daddy, Don Johnson. But prior to that day, I first needed to connect with my spiritual daddy, the one and only true living God. *God knows my past and loves me still.*

Ephesians 2:1–10: "And you hath he quickened, who were dead in trespasses and sins: wherein in time past ye walked according to the course of this world, according to the prince of the power of the air, the spirit that now worketh in the children of disobedience: among whom also we all had our conversation in times past in the lust of our flesh, fulfilling the desires of the flesh and of the mind; and by nature the children of wrath, even as others.

"But God, who is rich in mercy, for his great love wherewith he loved us, even when we were dead in sins, hath quickened us together with Christ, (by grace ye are saved;) and hath raised us up together, and made us sit together in heavenly places in Christ Jesus: that in the ages to come he might show the exceeding riches of his grace in his kindness toward us through Christ Jesus. For by grace are ye saved through faith; and that not of yourselves; it is the gift of God: not of works, least any man should boast. For we are his workmanship, created in Christ Jesus unto good works, which God hath before ordained that we should walk in them."

"The prince of the air" is Satan. "Satan" means adversary. "Adversary" means opponent, rival, or enemy against Christ or what Christ stands for. Satan is only the temporary ruler of the part of the world that chooses to follow him. The fact that all people, without exception, commit sin proves that we have a sinful nature. On God's absolute scale, no one is good. Only through uniting our lives with Christ's perfect life can we become good in God's sight. Christ is the permanent ruler of the whole world. The penalty of sin and its power over us were destroyed by Christ on the cross. Through faith in Christ we stand acquitted, or not guilty, before God (Romans 3:21, 22). We will still feel like sinning, and sometimes we will sin. The difference is that before we gave our life to Christ, we were dead in sin and slaves to our sinful nature, but now we are "quickened" with Christ (Galatians 2:20). Because of Christ's resurrection, we know that our bodies will be raised from the dead (1 Corinthians 15:2–23) and we have been given the power to live as true Christians now, today. (Ephesians 1:19) Our eternal life with Christ is certain, because we are united in his powerful victory. We become Christians through God's unmerited grace. We are not saved merely for our own benefit, but to serve Christ and build up the church. *God's intention is that our salvation will result in acts of service out of gratitude and love for him.*

Matthew 6:33: "But seek ye first the kingdom of God, and his righteousness and all things shall be added unto you."

To seek God, means to turn to him first for help, to fill your thoughts with his desires, to take his character for your pattern of how to live, and to serve and obey him in everything. You must actively choose to give God first place in all areas of your life.

Matthew 7:7–8: "Ask, and it shall be given you; seek, and you shall find; knock, and it shall be opened unto you: for every one that asketh receiveth; and he that seeketh findeth; and to him that knocketh it shall be opened."

Jesus tells us to persist in pursuing God. People often give up after a few halfhearted efforts and conclude that God cannot be found. Knowing God takes faith, focus, and follow-through, and Jesus assures us that our efforts will be rewarded. Do not give up in your efforts to seek God. Continue to ask him for more knowledge, patience, wisdom, love, and understanding.

I was now twenty-five and had been attending church for two years. I had learned enough to know that I needed a savior. With a child-like faith I took the first step and gave my life to Jesus on October third 1987, followed with baptism and the Lord's Supper on October eighteen 1987. My church family, my daughter, and Jim were present to witness this event. It was an amazing day and will be remembered and celebrated. *God knows, my limited knowledge and understanding and will help me to grow.*

The most important events in history are the death, burial, and resurrection of Jesus Christ, and his return to earth. Receiving Jesus, as your personal savior is the most valuable decision you will ever make. It carries profound significance far beyond our natural understanding. By trusting Jesus Christ as your savior, you become a son/daughter of God by being born again. The new birth is described in *John 1:12–13, "But as many as receive him [your decision to trust Christ as your savior], to them he gave the power to become the sons of God [your entrance into God's family], Which were born, not of blood, nor of the will of flesh, nor of the will of man [it is not a physical birth], but of God [it is a spiritual birth]."* Because of your new birth, you have inherited God's divine nature. You now have eternal life; you are not waiting for it sometime in the future. Your spiritual life is mentioned in present tense in these verses.

John 6:47: "He that believeth on me hath everlasting life."

John 3:36: "He that believeth on the Son hath everlasting life."

1 John 5:12: "He that hath the Son hath life."

2 Corinthians 5:17–18: "Therefore if any man be in Christ, he is a new creature: old things are passed away; behold, all things are become new. And all things are of God, who hath reconciled us to himself by Jesus Christ."

As a Christian, baptism and the Lord Supper are two ordinances practiced by the believer. Jesus left us these memorials to keep before us as a reminder of his sacrifice on the cross for our sins. Both ordinances commemorate the death, burial, and resurrection of the Lord Jesus Christ. Baptism is the first act of obedience for a believer. Baptism is *not* essential for salvation. Salvation is by grace through faith in the sacrifice of Jesus Christ on the cross. Nothing you do can be added to the grace of God for salvation, however the requirements of salvation and baptism are the same.

Romans 10:9–10: "That if thou shalt confess with thy mouth the Lord Jesus, and shalt believe in thine heart that God hath raised him from the dead, thou shalt be saved. For with the heart man believeth unto righteousness; and with the mouth confession is made unto salvation."

Baptism is essential for your spiritual growth. Jesus himself set the example by submitting to baptism before his ministry began (see Matthew 3; 13–17, Mark 1; 9–11, and Luke 3; 21–22). Your growth in Jesus Christ will be hindered if you will not obey a simple command of God.

The other ordinance a believer participates in is the Lords Supper. Like baptism, it is *not* essential for salvation, but it is very important for your growth in your new life with Jesus Christ. One of the primary reasons to observe the Lord Supper is for regular remembrance of the price Jesus paid for your sins, and it is a picture of his suffering. The bread is broken to remind you Jesus body was broken for your sins.

1 Corinthians 11:24: "And when he had given thanks, he brake it, and said, Take, eat: this is my body, which is broken for you: this do in remembrance of me."

The juice is "poured out" by drinking it to remind you that the blood of Jesus Christ was shed for your sins.

Matthew 26:27–28: "And he took the cup, and gave thanks, and gave it to them, saying Drink ye all of it; For this is my blood of the new testament, which is shed for many for the ransom of sins." There are three specific "views" you should take as you observe the Lord's Supper.

1. Past tense—To remind you of what Jesus did on the cross to pay for your sins.

2. Present tense—To judge your own sins.

3. Future tense—To anticipate his second coming.

Romans 6:4: "Therefore we are buried with him by baptism into death: that like Christ was raised up from the dead by the glory of the father, even so we also should walk in newness of life."

The day I received the Lord Jesus Christ as my personal savior, the Holy Spirit of God took up residency in my body. The Holy Spirit is God's personal presence in your life, and desires to produce a godly change as you *learn to walk* with him. With God's power now inside of me, I was open to learning and willing to be taught, but a few more years of my life would pass before I was able to grasp the concept: *I must do my part and be willing to make the time.* To get to know anyone on a personal level, you *must spend time* with the person. *God knows, my priorities are unbalanced, and working things out for me!*

I did feel a change within myself that day. I was filled with courage and strength to endure the situation in which I found my personal life. I returned home and played the role of a happy and content wife. Jim on the other hand had to go through a legal battle with law enforcement concerning tax evasion on his nightclub and was looking at possible jail time. To avoid prison, Jim released ownership of the club to the proper authorities and to avoid losing his house, Jim put the property into my name. *God knows, my future, and is working in this situation.*

I became pregnant again. This time with twins! By the time I was three months, I looked like I was full-term. I remember the pastor announcing my pregnancy to the church, and as the congregation applauded and congratulated Jim, I ran to the altar and bawled my eyes out. I started receiving prenatal care and after the doctor reviewed my medical history, he suggested I restrain from sexual activity until after the twins were born. This was great news to me and Jim had no choice but to agree to the request. I accepted the fact that I would soon be a mother to twins and began to rejoice in it. *God knows my emotions and is patient with me.*

A couple of my friends asked would I care for their children during the day while they worked. This was a great opportunity for me to be able to stay at home with my own children and continue to make an income. I quit my other job, got the house licensed for in-home childcare, and enrolled more children. In October 1988 I gave birth to my healthy and beautiful baby boys. With the birth of my sons, I got my tubes burned so not to have any more unexpected children and I learned to pray continually. *God knows, and smiled upon me as I learned how to pray.*

It took time for my body to heal after the delivery of twins and I was completely exhausted at the end of each day. My entire focus was on raising my children correctly and building up my business, which was at full capacity of fourteen children. I flatly refused to engage or participate in any sexual activity with Jim. We still slept in the same bed and most nights the children slept in-between us. I was very happy with this arrangement, and in time Jim gave up, left me alone and allowed me to rest in peace. I believe Jim found sexual companionship elsewhere. That behavior did not concern me at all. I was content in becoming a great mother and teacher to the children in my care. *God knows, and his love toward me is sufficient.*

Jim soon got a job with an area furniture company as a truck driver. This was a union job and provided great medical coverage for the family. Most nights Jim would be home but at times this job required out of city deliveries, thus requiring Jim to be gone for days. I began to handle all the responsibilities of the house, including financial. Unbeknown to Jim, I opened a private savings account and recorded the finances into two separate checkbooks. One for Jim's viewing and other with the true budget. Jim was a great father to his children but his treatment to me was awful. I felt like a piece of property and a prisoner within the home. I planned and waited for an opportunity to escape. That opportunity presented itself about one year later when Jim announced that he had taken an over-the-road delivery and would be gone for one week. *God knows, the intent of my heart and will work out what is best for me.*

While Jim was gone, I rented a small house about two miles away. I took and moved only what would be needed for the children and me to get a fresh start. I contacted all the families enrolled in the day care and all agreed to keep their children in my care. With my livelihood secured, I moved with my children, now age six, two and two into a new and safe environment. I planned to get a legal separation and in time divorce Jim. I waited two weeks and made contact with Jim. I found out that during that time Jim had returned home to discover his wife and children gone. He had hired a lawyer, filed for divorce, and charged me with kidnapping the children. I also got legal advice and told the lawyer about my abuse and the reason for my actions. I was informed that since there was no documentation of the abuse and since Jim had been the first parent to file for divorce, I would be facing a long ugly legal battle for the children. That the legal system would give sole custody to Jim and require me to pay him child support until all things were sorted out. The final outcome would be my word against his and at this time it did not look good for the children or me. I met with Jim and he told me that he would stop at nothing in destroying my business, livelihood, and reputation if I did not agree to return back to him. *God knows, the motive behind the action, gives strength where it is needed, and is working on the situation.*

I prayed to God, asking him to remove from me anything thing that should come in-between the Lord and I. Feeling defeated and seeing no other option the children and I did return. This bold step in fighting for my freedom did not go unrewarded. Upon returning back the divorce and kidnapping charges were dropped by Jim. The children were able to be with both mother and father. And I was filled with courage and a supernatural power to be able stand up for myself. *God knows, and does what is best for all of us.*

I had a desire to expand the business from an in-home day care to a large childcare facility. I applied for and received a full-ride scholarship at the community college. The degree I was pursuing was in social science. Alongside the necessary courses for this degree, I was offered three electives. I chose public speaking (to overcome my fear of standing in front of people and speaking on a subject with confidence). The second elective I chose was winning ways to speak (learning how to rearrange words to convey a message to the receiver in a positive way). The third elective course I chose was American Sign Language. This course was the most difficult of all my classes. (ASL is a visible language using your hands and body to paint a picture for a deaf or hard of hearing person.) Being determined to understand this language, I stepped way out of my comfort zone and chose to do my internship at the Kansas School for the Deaf. I spent one year in this environment and learned many skills and life-changing lessons from the teachers, staff, and children. I completed my education, received an associate degree in social science, and at the graduation received recognition and recommendation from many to pursue my desire of being an independent business owner. *God knows, and gives victories in life to those who push forward to greater things.*

Using the house property as collateral I secured a small business loan and purchased a building. Working hard, and spending a lot of time and energy on making the building into a safe and healthy environment for children, the state inspection was passed and I received a license to care for 186 children with 14 teachers and staff including myself. I named the childcare business As We Grow Childcare. This was a great accomplishment in my life and I was very proud of myself. *God knows, and rejoices with us in our successes.*

On the same day of the grand opening of As We Grow, Jim told me, doctors had informed him that he had terminal cancer and was given six months to get things in order. Choosing not to tell the children of his illness, Jim spent as much time as possible with them. Together, Jim and I completed a living will and got all funeral arrangements made. During Jim's last few weeks, a hospices agency came into the home to care for him. The agency recommended grieving classes for the children, which we attended together. *God knows, each individual heart and provides help in our time of need.*

On Jim's last night, I was awakened out of sleep with a gun pointed at my forehead. Startled but amazing calm I spoke to Jim about our children and what would happen to them if he were to pull the trigger. After a few minutes Jim lowered the gun and began to cry uncontrollably. He then confessed how he had purposely planed every negative event that had happened during the past fifteen years to unfold just as it had. He told me, "One day while working at the clubhouse I received a strange phone call from a woman. She told me about you. She said you were very attractive and gave me your address. I asked her why she was telling me these things, and she simply replied, 'You needed to be taught a lesson.' " I asked Jim, "Did this woman tell you who she was?" "No," he said, "she was just a voice on the other end of the line." I then spoke out loud the thought that had entered my mind. I said, "You have met my stepmother, Kara, do you think it was her?" "I honestly do not know, he replied and continued, what I do know however, is that ever since you and Renee left her house ten years ago, Kara has called and talked with me concerning you several times. I told her that I have fallen in love with you and my children. You and the kids are the only good and positive thing that has happened to me, and I never expected it. I have tried so hard to make you love me, but you never have and I can't bear the thought of you being with someone else after I'm gone. That's why I planned to kill you tonight. I do love you, Cindy. And you know I love Renee, Ron, and Stan. When you started talking about them, I knew you were right and I was wrong. I need you to forgive me for what I've done to you."

I listened carefully to every word of this confession. Jim told me he helped in the plans surrounding my kidnapping and rape. He admitted to knowing the taxi cab driver and the woman that had brought me to him. Again, Jim, asked me to please forgive him. I was in shock from the information I had just received and at the exact same time I was filled with compassion for Jim. I did not understand these confusing emotions and being spiritually immature, I could not form my words to say *I forgive you.* What I did tell Jim was that if anything had unfolded in any other way I would not have been blessed with our three beautiful children and for them I will be forever grateful. I assured him that I would raise our children up Christian and that God would provide the way. Jim suddenly vomited, took his last breath and died. *God knows, our most shameful secrets, extends mercy toward us and forgives us when we confess and repent.*

My mother Ellen attended Jim's funeral with me and her grandchildren. My mother had accepted and never asked any questions about my marriage with Jim. I never told her anything about my bondage and on that day I never wanted her to know the truth. It felt good to have my mother's love and support. I showed no visible emotion at Jim's funeral and truly believed that all my past pain, guilt, and shame was buried in the grave with him. *God knows, and in his time would reveal his plan for my life.*

About a week after Jim's passing, I received a card in the mailbox from Kara, signed, the Johnsons. I suddenly recalled receiving a card from Kara at the birth of my twins also, signed, the Johnsons. I did not give much thought to that action at that time, however this time I did think on it. The true fact is, I had never made contact with Kara in over ten years. I had never told her about the birth of my twins, nor had I told her about Jim's cancer. More thoughts began to fill my mind. Was Kara the woman's voice on the phone that had informed Jim of my whereabouts? Was that information provided responsible for my being kidnapped and raped? Was Kara aware of the time frame in my life as a prostitute and partly responsible for the past fifteen years of my life in bondage and captivity? Had Jim been encouraged to kill me before he died, leaving behind three small children, unable to care for themselves? We had never put in place our wishes concerning placement of our children should something happen to both of us. Our children would have become orphans and their future would have been determined by the court system. Kara and Dad would have been the closest surviving relatives of our children and would have been the court systems first choice of placement. What if Jim had pulled the trigger on the gun? What if my innocent children have fallen into the hands of their step-grandmother? I felt a cold chill run down my spine as I meditated on that thought.

I then turned the focus on myself. Why had I never given thought to this possibility before? How could I have been so stupid? Could evil truly be so powerful that it would pursue me throughout my life? I could not remain in this thought process. I needed to examine these thought patterns from a different perspective. I choose to think on the positive side. Today I am alive, healthy, and well able to provide for my children. Today I needed to become both mother and father for my children. I knew it would be a difficult road ahead, I would need lots of help along the way, and I knew I would have to grow up and except the help provided. *I could not let the scares of my past dictate what my future would hold. Today, I need to be strong and believe what the word of God says—I can do all things, through Christ, which strengthens me. God knows, our thoughts, and his way is greater than our way.*

2 Corinthians 10:3–6: "For though we walk in the flesh, we do not war against the flesh: for the weapons of our warfare are not carnal, but mighty through God to the pulling down of strong holds; casting down imaginations, and every high thing that exalteth itself against the knowledge of God, and bringing into captivity every thought to the obedience of Christ; and having in a readiness to revenge all disobedience, when your obedience is fulfilled."

We are weak humans, but we don't need to use human (carnal) plans and methods to win our battles, God's weapons are available to us to fight against Satan's "strongholds." The Christian must choose whose method to use, God's or the world's. God's mighty weapons— prayer, faith, hope, love, God's Word, and the Holy Spirit are powerful and effective (see Ephesians 6:13–18). These weapons break down the proud human arguments (strongholds) against God, and the walls Satan builds to keep people from finding God. When dealing with the pride that keeps people from finding Christ, we may be tempted to use our own methods. (Self-pride was a major stumbling block for me that will be discussed in the next section.) *Nothing can break down these barriers like God's weapons.*

I made some immediate changes in my life and the lives of my children. Using the funds now available to the children through Jim's death benefits, I enrolled all three into a private Christian school. I took out a second mortgage on the house, completely remolding both the inside and out. I expanded the footage of the layout and had it accredited and licensed by the state to provide care for children with special needs. This fulfilled a great need for the community in which I lived. I then closed the doors of the large As We Grow childcare center and reopened the day care inside the home. Because of the expansion the extra space legally allowed me to care for more children with an added adult. I decided on one of my most loyal employee and together we cared for a total of twenty-six children throughout each day. With state approval I was allowed to carry the same business name As We Grow childcare. In making these choices I was able to be both a stay at home mother to my children and finically provide for their needs. *God knows, our needs and provides a way.*

At the time of Jim's death I was thirty-three, my daughter was eleven and my twins had just had their seventh birthday. Over the next seven years things went well for the family. Our home was a place of laughter and love. All of us continued to grow spiritually and all three children excelled in sports, which in time, these skills provided full-ride scholarships to a college of their choice. During this time I also purchased a motorcycle, learned to ride, and joined the Christian Motorcycle Association. *God knows!*

When things in life are going well, people tend to forget to ask questions. *Why* is my life so good and who is making this possible? Like many others, I fell into the trap of deception and believed the lie that life was going well because of all the hard work I had put forth. I was looking at myself, and seeing my accomplishments, and saying to *self*, "Good job, *Cindy!*" *Self-pride* had entered into my unaware soul and taken root. It is true I had worked very hard toward the goals in my life. It is not true that I worked alone, nor did I alone deserve praise for my good works. *Why* my life was going well is because I had chosen to give control of my life to who? *Jesus!* The whole-truth is, the Holy Spirit gave me the strength and ability to accomplish what God had appointed, gifted, and ordained me to do.

God gave his Son, Jesus, who sent the Holy Spirit, who lives in me and empowers me to accomplish the things I do. I must remember I have a choice only because *Jesus first chose me*, and *I* live, *because Jesus lives.*

All praise and glory for my life, belongs only to God. God knows, I knew this to be true. What I did not know was *where, when,* and *how* to enter into a personal relationship with his Son, Jesus. *God reveals himself to me in many amazing ways.*

Life in the Wilderness and Asking the Right Questions

In 2002, with my daughter away at college and my sons busy with high school and sports, loneliness began to creep into my soul. Desiring companionship, I began to search for someone to fill this void. While attending a sporting event with my sons, I noticed the photographer taking the pictures. He was very attractive so I approached him and asked, "Are you married?" To which he responded, "No." I then extended my hand and introduced myself. To my surprise we carried the same last name. I then asked the second question, "Are we related?" To this question he stated, "No, I don't believe so." Exchanging business cards, I asked him to call me. Two weeks later I received a call and started dating this man. In a short time I became deeply involved with him. One day a woman informed me that this man was her husband and that he is fact was a married man!

At the time of this meeting I was saved and sealed by the Holy Ghost. I had the power living inside of me to ask the right questions and with spiritual wisdom discern the responses. I however, had not yet *learned how* to do this. Today, as I recalled this conversation, I know it was my own choice that placed me on a bad path. The first question asked, "Are you married?" The first word spoken, "No," was a lie. The second question asked, "Are we related?" The response, "No, I don't believe." With these words spoken, I should have turned, walked away and avoided much pain in the future. Words spoken are very powerful and will produce good or evil—depending on your choice. (Holy Spirit discernment is required to make the right choice.) I needed to *learn how* to hear *God's words* and *respond* properly. When you *respond* to any situation in life *take time to pray and ask God for his wisdom. God reveals himself through the power of words.*

Being spiritually immature *I reacted* improperly and blamed God for my bad choice. I was devastated by the news, using very angry words, I cried out to God. "How could you allow such a thing to happen to me? I'm a Christian doing many good works! My faith in you is shaken! Get my attention or I will just give up trying! If you really exist, you need to come here and visually show yourself to me! How dare you! Thump me on the head or something! I need proof to believe, you really are God!" *I decided I needed* to take a break to refocus on *my life* and started planning a two-week vacation. Destination Daytona Beach motorcycle rally. When you *react* to a situation in life *you say and do* what *feels* best for *self*, which often leads to another bad choice.

I got all things in order concerning the care of my sons and on February 22, 2002, I closed the doors of As We Grow for a period of two weeks. A girlfriend of mine suggested filling the tank of the bike prior to loading it on the trailer. I agreed and she rode on the backseat to the gas station. On the way I noticed a well-known biker friend on the side of the road and waved at him to follow us. At the station I told him of my Daytona Beach plans and asked if he would help in loading the bike on the trailer. He agreed to help and my girlfriend got on his bike for the return ride. Leaving the station, I took the lead. Scanning the road ahead, I noticed a slow moving vehicle in the left-hand lane. Slowing down myself, *I merged* into the right-hand lane, preparing to pass. Suddenly the vehicle turned right in front of me, clipping the front tire of the motorcycle, I lost balance, fall to the pavement and hit my head. I was not wearing a helmet and went unconscious. By ambulance I was taken to the trauma unit at an area hospital. I felt my spirit separating from my body. As my spirit floated upward, *I could hear* the conversation, and see the doctors trying to revive my body. My spirit continued to float upward and at the same time forward into a never-ending tunnel. Inside the tunnel *I was surrounded* by a thick, misty, gray, fog-like substance and *I felt completely helpless* to help myself. The only earthly experience in comparison to this feeling is when you are looking forward to spending a beautiful, fun-filled, sunny day at the park with family and friends, awake, run to the window full of excitement, looking out, see rain, and know that all your plans for the day must end.

Completely surrounded by this gray, misty substance *I continue forward.* I saw before me magnificent, huge gates slowing opening. The feeling inside me changed from helplessness to an overflowing comforting peace like I had never before felt. Jim, my deceased husband stepped out of the gates, stretching his hand forward, in the stop position. Looking at him, I shrugged my shoulders as if asking the question, "Why?" He then pointed to someone behind me. *I turned* my head, looking back and saw three children motioning for me to return. There was no mistaking the children as my own although all three were of younger days. Standing behind them, *I saw* the silhouette of a man. I did not recognize the man as anyone I personally knew but *I was immediately filled* with an unexplainable amount of hope. My thought—there is someone who loves my children and me. I looked back at Jim and said, "I love you." He said, "I forgive you."

I returned to the hospital room as the doctors were bringing me out of a drug-induced coma. To prevent any sudden movements my neck was braced, so all I could do was look up as my eyes started to focus. Leaning over me the doctor began asking several questions. "What's your name?" "C-i-n-d-y?" "How old are you?" "I don't know." "Do you know where you are?" "No." "Can you feel your legs?" "No, am I paralyzed?" "No," he responded, "your body is in shock, you are experiencing temporary paralyzes, you should have a full recovery. Do you remember the accident?" To this question, I asked the question, "Is my bike okay?"

I heard laughter and realized other people were in the room. I tried to sit up but could not. One by one everybody stood around the bed so I could see him or her. I recognized all the faces, but could not recall any names. A beautiful young woman and two very handsome boys appeared next to the bed and said, "You okay, Mama?" Renee! Don! Stan! *Thank you God! I remember* my children! Note the *italic* print: *I continued forward, I turned, I saw, I was immediately filled, Thank you God!*

I had been fully geared in leather at the time of the accident so I had little physical damage. I had no broken bones. I had only broken my fingernails, and chipped a tooth. A large patch of hair had been shaved off my forehead where I had received several stiches. My body was sore and it was difficult to raise my head, but the nurses quickly had me out of bed and moving about. I had knocked my equilibrium out of whack so I was unbalanced when I walked. Each step took total concentration. It looked and felt like I was stepping off the edge of a cliff. After a few days I was released and sent home to finish the recovery. I slept for hours at a time, often days, waking only to eat and walk short distances.

During this time I repeatedly had dreams and visions of the heavenly encounter I had received while in the coma. I asked myself many questions. *What* was the meaning of it? *Who* was the man standing behind my children? *Why* did I tell Jim I loved him, and why did he say I forgive you? While I was awake I sat for hours thinking and pondering the matters over and over again in my mind and could come up with no answer. I finally realized *I needed to ask God* for his help in understanding the vision. *I prayed* a short but very powerful prayer, *"Help me Lord, for I do not understand!"*

In God's time I received understanding to all my questions. I regained my short-term memory back quickly, but much more time would pass before I received back my long-term memory. To see how, when and where God's plan for my life was unfolded to be used for his glory please continue forward.

John 8:7, 10, 11: "So when they continued asking him, he lifted up himself, and said unto them, He that is without sin among you, let him first cast a stone at her. When Jesus had lifted up himself, and saw none but the woman, he said unto her, Woman, where are those thine accusers? Hath no man condemned thee? She said, No man,

Lord. And Jesus said unto her, Neither do I condemn thee: go, and sin no more."

This passage is found in the Bible in the short but powerful story of Jesus forgives an adulterous woman. (John 8:1–11). When others are caught in sin, are you quick to pass judgment? To do so is to act as though you have never sinned. It is God's role to judge, not ours. Our role is to show forgiveness and compassion. When Jesus said that only someone who had not sinned should cast the first stone, people slipped quietly away, from the eldest to the youngest. Evidently the older men were more aware of their sins than the young. Age and experience often temper youthful self-righteousness. But whatever your age, take an honest look at your life. Recognize your sinful nature, and look for ways to help others rather than hurt them.

My biker friend who had witnessed the accident came to visit and told me an amazing story about what he has seen just moments before the accident. He told me a big invisible bubble was all around the accident and the clouds in the sky began rolling. A wisp come out of the clouds and formed into the shape of a hand. When I hit the backside of the car the motorcycle stayed upright, and the hand caught my body and gently floated me to the ground. I then simply bumped my head on the pavement. The motorcycle then fell in the opposite direction away from my body. It appeared as if the scene of the accident was frozen in time and space. I then asked my girlfriend, his passenger, her version of what she had seen. She told me a similar story adding that the biker kept screaming at her to get off the bike, but she could not because they were still moving. She said, "*It was so surreal.*"

Ephesians 1:3, 5, 9, 11–12: "Blessed be the God and Father of our Lord Jesus Christ, who hath blessed us with all spiritual blessings in the heavenly places in Christ: having predestinated us unto the adoption of the children by Jesus Christ to himself, according to the good pleasure of his will, having made known unto us the mystery of his will, according to his good pleasure which he hath purposed in himself: in whom also we have obtained an inheritance, being predestinated according to the purpose of him who worketh all things after the counsel of his own will: that we should be to the praise of his glory, who first trusted in Christ."

"All spiritual blessings in heavenly places" means all the good things God give us—salvation, the gifts of the spirit, power to do God's will, and the hope of living forever with Christ. "Predestinated" means marked out beforehand. (Salvation is God's work—not our own doing.) "The mystery of his will" honestly, I do not fully understand, but *God's plan for the world could not be fully understood until Christ rose from the dead.* Many people do not understand God's plan for their life. Why things unfold as they do. Most times it is when you reflect on the things that are already in the past, set your mind on things in the present, and make goals with positive choices in your future that you *will begin to understand* the mystery of God's will for your life. When your life seems chaotic, rest in this truth: God's purpose to save you cannot be thwarted, no matter what Satan may bring. *Jesus is Lord, and God is in control.*

God blessed me with an amazing daughter. Renee had been away at college at the time of the accident. She immediately requested and was granted time away from her studies in order to return home to care for her mother. She made the drive and was at the hospital when I woke up. Renee reopened the childcare business, paid the bills, looked after her brothers, and took care of any other responsibilities that arose. Since I was so unstable she brushed my hair, helped me to eat, bathe, and get dressed. My physical body was still in pain due to the impact of the accident so Renee took me to the family physician and requested a pain prescription. Hydrocodone was prescribed. My medical history reveals the fact that I am highly allergic to codeine. Overlooked by the doctor, and unbeknown to me, I started taking this codeine-based drug for pain. Several weeks later I developed hives, boils, deep-rooted sores, and had become very sensitive to sunlight. My body temperature increased to dangerously high levels and I was experiencing migraine headaches. To relieve the itching and lower the temperature I would submerge my body into a tub of cold water and Renee would add buckets of ice cubes. I wrapped my arms and legs in soft gauze overlaid with bandages to prevent the spreading of the boils and sores. The location and placement of the sores was strange. It was as if though my body could be divided in half and if I got a sore on the right side, you would be sure to find a sore on the opposite side of my body in the same location. One day I walk from the house to the mailbox barefoot (only a few feet) and instantly the bottom of my feet were covered with boils. I had also developed a strange butterfly shaped rash on my face. I was so miserable that Renee took me to the emergency room. I was admitted to the hospital and many test were taken. Through x-rays it was discovered that my internal organs had slowly began shutting down. The first major concern was the small intestines, which had pinhole size lesions and was releasing poisonous fluid into the bloodstream. None of the doctors examining me were able to tell what was wrong or why my body was under attack.

A well-known skin specialist was contacted to review my case. When she arrived, she took one look at my face and stated, "You have lupus." She examined the medical charts and very confident in her decisions, turned to the nurses and began giving orders. "Stop that, start this, and get an IV of steroids into this body." The nurses obeyed all the orders without question. I was thankful to have a diagnosis of my condition but not having a clue to what it is, I asked, "What is lupus?" Not answering my question, she began asking her own. "*Do you have someone to live for?*" Puzzled by her question, I frankly stated, "My children." "That's as good of place to start as any I suppose," looking at the half empty IV she continued, "*Are you feeling better?*" Surprised, I responded, "Yes! I do feel much better, I'm not itching anymore!" She then examined my body. The hives and facial rash were disappearing right before our eyes. She extended her hand and introduced herself. "My name is Dr. Waxman, be in my office at 8:00 a.m. sharp, don't be late, or I will have to pass you over and you may not get another chance to get in. *I'm always on time* and I don't waste my patient's time."

She then asked what I thought at the time to be a very strange question, "*Do you tan?*" "I have in the past," I replied. "Stop," she stated, "*If God wanted you to have dark skin, He would have created you that way.*" Turning her attention back to the nurses, she told them after the IV has run its course, release this woman into my care.

She then turned to exit, stopped at the door, with a face displaying concern; she seemed to have received an afterthought. Looking back at me, in a voice full of compassion, she stated, *"Don't listen to what anyone else tells you about lupus,"* then changing her voice to a matter of fact tone she finished her thought, *"my patients live long and productive lives."*

After she left I asked the nurse, "What exactly is lupus." I was told that lupus is a chronic illness that attacks the immune system. There is no known cure to this disease, and many people die from the complications related to lupus. I left the hospital with this information rolling over and over again in my mind. While driving home I turned the radio to a Christian station, every song was about forgiveness. I asked God, "What do I need forgiveness for? I'm a good person! I love you! I can't die! Who will care for my children?" As I pulled the car into my driveway, another song played across the airwaves. I had never before heard this particular song. It was "You're an Overcomer" by Mandisa. I did not have any knowledge or understanding of why I was going through these things, but I did know that God had always taken care of my children and me. I thought on the entire blessings we had received in the past years. I knew about God's promise to never leave or forsake us. *I needed to learn how to truly trust God with my life!*

What exactly do I mean by that statement? Do I not already trust God with my life? I thought I did! Let's take a moment to take a deeper look at the questions Lisa asked and the statements she made: *(1) Do you have someone to live for? (2) Are you feeling better? (3) Do you tan? Stop, if God wanted you to have dark skin, he would have created you that way! (4) Don't listen to what others say about your condition! (5) My patients live long and productive lives!*

Now, let's take a look at my *reaction* to the questions at the time versus my response today!

1. My reaction to the question, my children, is a good answer, but not the correct one. Today, I know the correct response to the question is, I live for God!

2. Yes, I am feeling better—today, I understand why I felt better—the correct medicine was going into my system (veins)! Today, the correct medicine is the Word of God!

3. Stop! Trying to look and be like other people, God uniquely created me and (you) different. God loves and accepts us just the way we are, even in our weakness.

4. Don't just listen to other opinions, search for the correct answers for yourself! You must move past exposure to the Word, to studying the Word of God for yourself!

5. People who live for God, will live productive lives! People who truly take the time to get to *know you, will know who you serve and that God is truly present in your life!*

At the time Lisa asked me these questions I was saved, I loved, and thought I trusted God with my life. However, there was no evidence in my life that produced an outward appearance that I had made this personal decision.

Because of my past, I trusted no one with my life. How could I truly trust in a Spirit I cannot see? Or had I? And just *did not yet know* I had!

Only time and more life experiences would reveal the deeper truth to my own questions!

I arrived at Dr. Waxman's office at 7:45 a.m. True to her word I was called back at 8:00 a.m. sharp. Preferring to use first name basis when talking with her patients, she told me she already knew my name and her name is Lisa. She identified herself to be Christian and truly believed God had blessed her in serving people, in the area of medicine. She continued on saying, "Although, there was much sacrifice of my time to study, it was all worth it, when I received my diploma." If you put your faith in God, and do all I tell you to do, you will be okay no matter what the outcome. *"Do you understand* what I'm saying?" I started to respond, "Yes, but." Holding up her hand to stop me from completing the statement, she gently said, "The answer is yes, you understand, do not add anything else to your statement. Life or death is in the power of the tongue. *Chose to speak life over yourself and healing will follow!"* Lisa did several biopsies on the sores, explaining that it would be sent to a lab and we would have to wait for the results. She told me of some lifestyle changes I needed to commit to. Daily recording the information and progress I was making, and she wanted to continue seeing me on a weekly basis. *God reveals himself, through words spoken by other believers.*

I did all Lisa prescribed and in time my physical body healed. All the hives, rashes, sores, boils, and blisters dried up and faded away, leaving only a few almost unnoticeable scares. *A well-known doctor was appointed to my internal issue* concerning the lesions on my small intestines.

Several weeks had passed since I last attended church. I now was feeling much better physically but I had become spiritually starved for God's word, so I attended a Sunday evening service. Unbeknown to me at the time, our regular pastor was not speaking and a guest speaker was introduced. Prophet Rob was his name. This man had a look all his own. I'm not saying this as to in anyway offend, but simply stating, "Don't judge a book (look) by its cover." Rob proudly wore the brightest red mohawk I have ever seen and in my opinion, his style of clothing was a bit questionable. *He was not who you would except to see in the pulpit anointed by God.*

He spoke boldly the truth and promises of the Lord. He called forward many members, placed his hands on them, and spoke healing over them. Suddenly he faced the congregation and said, "There certainly are a lot of knuckleheads here tonight." I repositioned myself in the pew, unbuttoned the collar of my blouse and peeked at my undergarment. Across the top of my T-shirt was the word knucklehead. I tilted forward; listening to every word he spoke to others, claiming them as my own. When the service finished and as he was preparing to exit the sanctuary, I stood to my feet, and said out loud, "Your words are powerful and true."

Never looking to see who had made the statement he stopped, and said, "You cannot just reach out for it as you drive by, *you must walk the land and place your hands upon it.*" Startled by his response, I sat down in the pew and prayed until the church was near empty. I had no idea what he meant by his words. I returned home, unable to sleep, I continued to pray throughout the night. The next morning I received a call from my doctor. In a bewildered voice I heard, "Cindy, I don't know what it is you are doing but keep it up. I'm standing here reviewing your most recent x-rays. There are no lesions, no scare tissue, as a matter of fact, there is no signs that lupus ever existed in your body." Today, I still do the necessary things to keep the lupus in remission, but I'm able to enjoy a healthy lifestyle in the sunshine including riding my motorcycle. As previously stated, *a well-known doctor was appointed to my internal issues—God reveals himself through unexplainable healings.*

Luke 17:15–16, 19: "And one of them, when he saw that he was healed, turned back, and with a loud voice glorified God, and fall down on is face at his feet, giving him thanks: and he was a Samaritan. And he said unto him, Arise, go thy way: thy faith hath made thee whole."

This passage is found in the short, yet powerful story of Jesus heals ten lepers (Luke 17:11–19). The people in the story are lepers, and were required to stay apart from other people. Ten were healed but only one thanked him. Not only was the thankful one a leper, he was also a Samaritan. A race of people despised by the Jews as idolatrous half-breeds.

God's grace is for everyone. I was a child, unwanted and unloved. I was a stripper, a prostitute, a woman filled with shame and guilt. Yet God loved me, forgave me, and healed my broken body. How could I do anything less than continue on this road, no matter where it leads, no matter what I must go through or however long it takes. Only grateful Christians grow in understanding of God's grace. It is possible to receive God's great gifts with an ungrateful spirit. God does not demand that we thank him, but he is pleased when we do so, and he uses our responsiveness to teach us more about himself. *God reveals himself, through our responsiveness to him.*

At this point in my story I want to take a moment to speak to you reading this book *I believe* when speaking of the power of God, *it is wise not to use words like never and always.* To do so would suggest limiting God's ability to our own human understanding. God speaks to his children in a variety of countless ways. God is the creator of the universe. God knows all about you. After all he created you and nothing you have ever done or ever will do is a surprise to God. God chose to reveal his truth to me through his Word and continual communication with him in prayer. With testimonies of other people, several different study books, music, songs, worship, and dreams and visions, just to name a few. When you make the decision to submit all areas of your life to God's control, he will use every bit of your life for his glory. In the next few pages I will tell only of a few life-changing events that took place. There are not enough pages in this book to contain all the mighty miracles God has done in my life. All these things done were preceded with much prayer, deep Bible study, a strong leading of the Holy Spirit and concluded with confirmation from God.

In time the desire for a companion returned. This time however, I chose a different approach in fulfilling the desire. *I prayed!* I gave the desire to the Lord, *trusting in him* to know what was best for me. God's word says; we are not to settle for anything less than the very best he has for us. A few weeks later, while sitting on the toilet in a public restroom, I was thinking about how wonderful life would be with someone who really loved me for just being me. Suddenly I heard a *loud voice* say, "MARRY ME!" Startled, I bent down and looked under the stall expecting to see feet. I saw no other feet, out loud I said, "Who said that?" Again in a *loud voice*, I heard, "MARRY ME FIRST, I HAVE MANY THINGS TO SHOW YOU!" Looking up I questioned, "God, is that you?" There was no reply. Completely puzzled and still looking up, I stated, "No offense, God, I love you and all that, but what I really want is a physical man." Again there was no reply. I got up and walked outside. I looked at the sunrise, smelled the aroma in the air, and listened to the birds chirping. *All of my senses seemed to have been greatly enhanced.* There was no rationalizing what I had just experienced. God is the creator of the universe. God loves me and he cares for even the smallest concerns in my life. *God reveals himself in supernatural ways.*

Hebrews 2:1–4 Therefore we ought to give the more earnest heed to the things which we have heard, least at any time we should let them slip. For if the word spoken by angels was steadfast, and every transgression and disobedience received a just reward; how shall we escape, if we neglect so great salvation; which at first began to be spoken by the Lord, and was confirmed unto us by them that heard him; God also bearing witness, both with signs and wonders, and with divers (various) miracles, and gifts of the Holy Ghost, according to his own will.

This scripture tells us to listen carefully (give the more earnest heed) to the truth they have heard so not to drift away into false teachings. Listening is hard work. It involves focusing our minds, bodies, and senses. Listening to Christ means not merely hearing but also obeying. We must listen carefully and be ready to carry out his instructions. "The words spoken by angels" refers to the teaching that angels, as messengers for God, brought the Law to Moses (see Galatians 3:19). Just as Christ is greater than angels, so his message is more important than theirs. We have not seen Christ in the flesh, but we base our belief in Jesus on eyewitness accounts recorded in the Bible. "God also bearing them witness" continues this thought. Those who heard Jesus—speak and passed on his words were true by "signs and wonders, and with diverse miracles, and gifts of the Holy Ghost." Gifts of the Spirit authenticated the Gospel wherever it was preached. The purpose of spiritual gifts is to build up the church, making it strong and mature. When we see the gifts of the Spirit in an individual or congregation, we know God is truly present. As we receive his gifts, we should *thank him* for them and put them to use in the church. *All Gospel preached should point to Jesus Christ as the only way to salvation.*

I returned home and *continued to pray*. I entered into *deep prayer*, deeper than I had ever been before. I lay face down, with my body as flat as I could go upon the carpet. Crying uncontrollably I receive a vision from God. In the vision I saw my Lord and Savior carrying the cross to Calvary. A short distance behind Jesus, I saw myself also carrying a cross. I saw the entire experience including the painful nailing to the cross and the shameful lifting up of Jesus. During this time in the vision, I saw myself kneeling at the foot of my Lord's cross rising up my arms and begging for his forgiveness of my sins. Jesus looked down at me and said, "Forgive her Father, for she knows not what she is doing." The vision ended—the carpet was soaked with my tears. I arose and went to the bathroom to wash my face. Looking at myself in the mirror, I noticed the cross I always wear around my neck was missing. The chain was unbroken but the solid gold cross with a small stone in the middle was not there. I lifted up my arms and cried out to God, *"Please Lord not my cross, it means so much to me, please give me back my cross."* Being led by the Spirit, I walked out of the bathroom, down the stairs, across the family room and stood before the large white rock fireplace located in the center of my home. Kneeling down I began prying loose the carpet that was being held tight in place by the tack strip. I pulled the carpet back about two or three inches and found my cross. Like I mentioned earlier the cross is made of solid gold and the chain around my neck was unbroken. There was no way humanly possible for this to have happened. I put the cross back on the chain, rose to my feet and said, *"What would you have me to do Lord?"* Instantly I heard the Lord speak to my spirit, *"Give back to me your time and speak only the truth."* I did not understand, I thought to myself, I go to church and Bible study, and I do not purposely lie to anyone. *What does the Lord mean?"*

I called together a family meeting. All three of my children and my future daughter-in-law listened to everything I had to say, starting with *"things around here are going to change"* and finishing the conversation with the statement, "I'm lonely and I'm in prayer for a husband." My daughter responded first stating, "Mom, I'm an adult now, I'm starting a family of my own, you do what is best for yourself and know that I love you and will support any decision you make." My twin sons in unison replied," It's about time, Mom, we're sick and tired of you trying to control our lives." This was as close to a heartfelt statement I was going to receive from my children at this time in their lives, so I grasped their approval of my decision as a blessing from God.

Turning to my future daughter-in-law I said, "I plan to rededicate my life to God in the morning, will you attend church with me?" She smiled at me and stated, "I would be honored to be by your side on such an important event in your life." Kelly is her name and I pray that my son's eyes would be opened to see this amazing young woman God has placed into his life. Early the next morning,

I walked into my closet in search for something to wear. Hanging in the back corner still in plastic wrapping was a beautiful white dress that I had purchased about one year ago in anticipation of my wedding day. *This is a good day; I will rejoice and be glad in it,* I thought to myself as I put on the dress for the first time. Kelly arrived and together we went to church. The message was very appropriate; the pastor spoke on being single, rather young or widowed, wait upon the Lord. It is better to be alone, than to be married to the wrong person. God can use the lives of single people in a mighty way, for they can devote their entire life to him without having other distractions to pull them away. I thought to myself, I fit into both categories, I'm a widow and at this time in my life I'm also a single woman in prayer for a companion. At the end of the service I approached the altar and humbly *gave all areas of my life to God's control.*

Kelly also gave her life and asked Jesus to live within her. Pastor spoke with Kelly and walked with her through the sinner's prayer. After Kelly affirmed that she understood her decision to give her life to Jesus, Pastor turned his attention to me, stating, "You look very pretty, I guess you're not riding your bike today!" "Thank you, Pastor," I replied, "*You married me to God today.*" Extending his hand and shaking mine, he firmly stated, "*Welcome to the Kingdom!*" He then turned and picked up a Bible lying on the altar that was intended for the guests that had attended the service this day. Placing it into my hands he gently said, "Read this." I started to protest because I already owned a Bible, but instead I read the cover, Life Application Study Bible, KJV. Now at age forty-four, I had been a professing Christian for over twenty years, I had attended church and Bible study on a regular basis but the one thing I had never done was read and study the Bible for myself. Taking the gift, thanking Pastor, I smiled and said, "*I will.*"

The Bible is the greatest book ever written to the human race throughout history. The Application Bible does what a good resource Bible should—it helps you understand the context of a passage, gives important background and historical information, explains difficult words and phrases, and helps you see the interrelationships within Scripture. The Life Application Bible also goes deeper into God's

Word, helping you discover the timeless truth being communicated, see the relevance for your life, and make a personal application. Application is deeply personal—unique for each individual. It is making a relevant truth a personal truth, and it involves developing a strategy and action plan to live in harmony with the Bible. It is the biblical "how to" of life. This is a great resource Bible and I highly recommend it to any student of the Word of God.

Several times in the past I had tried to read and always struggled with understanding the Bible. Due to the brain trauma I received at the time of the motorcycle accident, I had a very difficult time retaining information and I had very few memories of my past or what type of life I had lived thus far. *To live correctly in the present and move forward into the future, I needed healing of the past. God reveals himself in His book, the Bible.*

To find answers I decided to meet with my pastor's wife. Starting with the most recent event and going backward, I told her all I could remember back to the motorcycle accident. Everything prior to the accident, I had no memory of. Having been my friend for several years, she reminded me of major events that she was personally aware of. Knowing I was still confused, she suggested I visit the gravesite of my deceased husband and father of our children; to the best of my recollection, something I had not done since his death. On the way to the gravesite, I recalled the words spoken by Prophet Rob, *"You cannot just reach out for it as you drive by, you must walk the land and place your hands upon it"* It had been over ten years since Jim lost his battle with cancer. I had been very busy with raising our children and operating a business. I had driven by the graveyard at least once a week but never felt the need to enter in. As I thought on these things and spoke with the Lord, *a feeling of expectation began filling my soul. I was certain the Lord was with me and he would help me to understand.*

As I entered the graveyard the first thing I noticed was how well kept the property was. It was beautifully landscaped. Large trees lined the road I was traveling on. At the time Jim's body was laid to rest the area located in the far northeast corner was undeveloped. I parked my motorcycle and started down the walkway toward Jim's grave. I heard wind chimes and my attention was drawn to the sound. Looking around I spotted the chimes; also surrounded by large balloons. Curiosity caused me to leave the walkway and I headed in the direction of the chimes. Along the way I stopped many times to read the name and date inscribed on the headstones. I wondered about the lives of these people and what stories they could tell. When I reached the gravesite with the wind chimes and balloons, I noticed the loose dirt indicating a recent burial. At the base of the headstone were freshly planted rosebushes and a framed photograph of a beautiful child. Reading the inscription and doing the math I knew the body of a nine-year-old child lay resting. Not knowing anything about what circumstances this child had gone through during her short life, I began grieving with her parents for the loss of their precious gift from God. I cannot even begin to imagine the pain of losing one of my own children. I prayed for healing in her parents and rejoicing in the good moments and memories during this child's short-allotted time spent here on earth. I continued across the land headed toward my own destination thinking, *life is but a moment in time compared to eternity.*

Reaching Jim's gravesite, I kneeled down and began pulling away the weeds that had grown at the base of his headstone. I picked up and replanted a wreath that had been blown over by the wind. The banner on the wreath read, "In memory of our beloved father, your children." I recalled the situation my children were in at the time they truly grieved their father. My daughter was away at college, calling to tell me the wonderful news about a young man she had met and was planning to one day marry. Her joy turned to sorrow as she realized and said, "My daddy won't be here to walk me down the aisle." To comfort my daughter, I responded, "I would be honored to walk you, sweetheart." The moment for my twin sons was after returning home from a basketball tournament; talking proudly about their high scoring ability, how they had stood before the crowd of people and received recognition by their coaches for their skill and talent. They both broke down and wept, saying, "I wish Dad could have been here and seen this." I reassured them that as long as they carried their father in their heart, he was aware of their gifts, talents, and accomplishments.

At the time my response to my children seemed good and right. They knew nothing about the abuse their father had inflicted upon their mother. I had never spoken one bad word to the children concerning their father. At the time of their father's passing, they were too young and no good would have come of it. As a matter of fact: I had never told anyone of the abuse I had endured. As I reflected on my life, memories of the years spent with Jim, began rolling through my mind. I remembered the shame and guilt I had felt during that time and how I behaved after his funeral. In my life I had a sense of newfound freedom. I had not properly considered and handled what my children were going through. No matter how their father had treated their mother, my children truly loved him and he in return loved them. Realizing this great truth for the first time and realizing that I also had made bad choices affecting the lives of my children, I spoke out loud, *"What am I to do about it!"* Scriptures entered my mind.

Ephesians 6:12: "For we wrestle not against the flesh and blood, but against principalities, against powers, against rulers of the darkness of this world, against spiritual wickedness in high places."

Matthew 7:1: *"Judge not,* that ye be not judged."

1 Peter 3:17–18: "For it is better, if the will of God be so, that if ye suffer for well doing, than for evil doing. For Christ also suffered for sins, the just and the unjust, that he might bring us to God, being put to death in the flesh, but quickened by the spirit."

At that moment I received this vision from the Lord; I saw myself traveling down a long, dry, dusty gravel road. Stopping at the fork in the road, I looked to the left; it was a wide road with lots of people standing on both sides calling for me to come this way. In the distance I saw death and destruction of many family members and friends. I looked to the right; it was a long, narrow, winding path. In the distance, high on a mountaintop was a brilliantly bright cross. I saw my children dancing and many grandchildren playing around the foot of it. There were many mountaintops and many valleys in-between the cross and myself. I could not see what lies in the valleys or how far they stretched. What I would have to go through or how long it would take. All I could see for certain is the cross at the finish. I heard the Lord speak to my spirit asking, *"Will you carry your cross of accountability, walk with me, and be my disciple?"* My answer is *"Yes, Lord, yes, yes, Lord. I will do all you ask of me!"* I chose the long, narrow, winding path. *I chose the right path. The path less traveled.*

I truly believe what took place inside of me this day at the graveyard was a spiritual indwelling of Christ. This is called conversion; the sinner comes to Christ, not Christ to the sinner; and the sinner's conversion is the work of the Holy Spirit, and not the work of Christ. In the believer, it will produce an outward, visible, personal coming. I had been told many times by other believers that I had the hand of God upon me. This day I knew those words to be true. I not only felt the hand of God upon me, I felt God's presence all around and through me. *God reveals himself, in personal and intimate ways.*

I returned home. Picked up the Bible. Starting in Genesis, reading, studying, and meditating on every scripture, verse, and word. I purchased Dispensational Truth by Clarence Larkin to help in my understanding of spiritual warfare, the dispensations, the times and the ages. I read many books containing personal testimonies of people who have gone through similar experiences. I wrote down all my thoughts and all my learning. I devoted many hours, every day to prayer and study. Finishing in Revelation I discovered the Bible is complex and so simple a child can understand at the exact same time. *God reveals himself, when we take the time, to learn of Him.*

The first life-changing thing I did was announcing that I would be closing the doors to my business, As We Grow Childcare. This facility was a Christian base ministry serving low income, underprivileged, special needs children and families. I had owned and operated this facility for nearly twenty-five years. I loved my work and thanked God for the joy I had experienced during that season in my life. This business had been the greatest source of my income, and had provided well for the financial needs of my family. Walking away from my livelihood, in order to devote my time to study required faith in trusting God to provide for all my needs. This was a very difficult decision in my life, for I knew not what God's plan for my future was to be. *I asked God, "Why?"*

Matthew 17:20–21: "And Jesus said, Because of your unbelief: for verily I say unto you, If ye have faith as a grain of mustard seed, ye shall say unto this mountain, Remove hence to yonder place; and nothing shall be impossible unto you. Howbeit this kind goeth not out but by prayer and fasting."

Jesus wasn't condemning the disciples for substandard faith; he was trying to show how important faith would be in their future ministry. If you are facing a problem that seems as big and immovable as a mountain, turn your eyes from the mountain and look to Christ for more faith. Only then will you be able to overcome the obstacles that stand in your way. Jesus was teaching that some work for God is more difficult than others and requires a greater than usual dependence on God. This verse does not mean that prayer and fasting alone would have accomplished the miracle. *Prayer and fasting indicate faith, discipline, and humility before God, without which there can be no hope of success.*

In making this decision I knew I would no longer be able to support the lifestyle in which I had come accustom to. I cut up all charge cards in order to not be tempted to spend. I returned all items I had previously purchased that I still owed a balance on. I made contact with my daughter who had returned home from college and was starting a family of her own, telling her, "Come and take anything in this house you need or want for your own." Renee took for her own all major appliances, furniture, and many small items to decorate her home. I felt good inside knowing my daughter had received *a blessing from God* in getting a fresh start in her life. I packed the personal things I would need. Not knowing where God would lead me I packed very light, about twelve boxes. Having many things still remaining, especially in the area of childcare equipment, I put up a sign stating, Everything Free.

I sat on the lawn with my grandson watching all I had owned being taken away by the truckloads. Although everything was free, *God had placed upon the hearts of many to give money.* Placing 20s, 50s, and 100s into my hands. At the end of the day I had more than enough to survive for some time. I then contacted a relator and placed my house up for sale. At the completion of this process, *I thanked God and waited for his instruction on what to do next.* A short time later, after receiving a powerful dream I was awaken from my sleep hearing a voice saying, *"As I tested my son Abraham, so I test you. Well done my child. I give to you the gift of faith."* *God reveals himself to an obedient heart.*

Hebrews 11:1: *"Now faith* is the substance of things hoped for, the evidence of things not seen."

Two words describe our faith: confidence and certainty. These two qualities need a secure beginning and ending point. The beginning point of faith is believing in God's character—he is who he says. The end point is believing in God's promises—he will do what he says. When we believe that God will fulfill his promises even though we don't see those promises materializing, we demonstrate true faith.

Faith is one component of the fruit of the spirit. At the time a believer confesses with the mouth and believes in the heart that Jesus is Lord, the Holy Spirit enters into the body and all the fruit of the spirit is planted into the good soil of the heart.

The gift of faith is an extra amount given to the believer by God in order to be used by God to fulfill his purpose and his will in your life. *I thanked God for the gift of faith; nothing can be accomplished without faith.*

God also spoke, "As I tested Abraham, so I test you." These words moved me to do a deep study on the life of Abraham. I knew there would be more tests to come. We all know there are consequences to any action we take. Unfortunately, when we are making a decision most of us think only of the immediate consequences. These are often misleading because they are short lived. You probably don't know the long-term effects of most decisions you make. But shouldn't the fact that there will be long-term results cause you to think carefully and seek God's guidance as you make choices and take action today?

The details of Abraham's life are found in Genesis in the Bible. Abraham had many strengths and accomplishments. Abraham also had many weaknesses, as all human's do. The key verse that I believe best describes Abraham's life is

Genesis 15:6: "And he believed in the LORD; and God counted it to him for righteousness"

It was Abraham's belief in the Lord, not his actions that made him right with God. Our outward actions—church attendance, prayer, and good deeds—will not by themselves make us right with God. A right relationship is based on faith—the heartfelt inner confidence that God is who he says he is and will do what he says he will do. Abraham was human and sinful. Abraham made mistakes. It was faith, not perfection that made him right in God's eyes. This principle holds true for us: *when we believe in God, he declares us righteous.*

Once As We Grow Childcare was closed, I had no immediate responsibilities to attend to. I reactivated my cosmetology license and did an apprenticeship under a skilled barber learning how to use the latest tools of the trade and updating the most current hairstyles. I got a job cutting hair three days a week, providing enough income to support my daily needs. Although I still owned my large house, I decided to move into a small two-bedroom rental. I did this because living in a big empty house all by myself gave me time to think about how really lonely I truly was. I needed to relocate so I could stay focused on what was most important at this time in my life: studying the Word of God.

Friends brought small appliances, furniture, bedroom sets, and so much food the cabinets were full to overflowing. I did not have a garage so I parked my motorcycle in the living room. I was very comfortable in my little space. When my twin sons returned home from college for a short visit, they were stunned at all the changes. They lovingly said, "Mom, we think you're nuts, but we love you anyway." I reminded them that their sister only lived two blocks away and for the most part they would have the entire space to themselves because I planned to stay at a place called the Healing House for a short time.

I had heard of the Healing House from one of my clients while cutting his hair. He was a personal friend of the owner and arranged a time for us to meet. At the meeting of Bobby-Jo, I discovered her to be very transparent about her past. She stated, "That by God's good grace, she had been rescued and lifted up from an abusive and troublesome past. A desire had been planted in her heart to provide a safe house for others traveling through what she herself had overcome."

I told her, "*I truly believe God had directed me to her for a reason. Although I had no understanding of what and why, I did know I was in training for something that was to take place in my future.*" All the women staying in one of Bobby-Jo's safe houses were going through and putting back together their lives that had been broken due to bad choices or decisions. The Healing House itself consisted of several houses that had been beautifully remolded and furnished to provide an atmosphere of peace and warmth. There was an apartment complex that had one or two bedrooms for mothers with small children. There was also a large building used as a gathering place for Bible study and personal testimonies. The Healing House main purpose was to introduce biblical principles and Christian living to its residents.

Although I had a place of my own, I asked Bobby-Jo if I could stay with the other women. She had limited space but agreed to let me take up residency at a house called The Sunshine House. This house was provided to women who had completed the program and were in process of reentering society. They all had jobs and different personal family connections. The second life-changing event happened during my seven-month stay at the Healing House. As not to appear any better than anyone else, I dressed in sweat suits, pulled my hair into a ponytail, and wore no makeup. I shared meals, work responsibilities, attended Bible study and church, and slept at the Sunshine House. I left only for work or to visit my own church. I quickly became friends with many of the women. I looked for ways in which I could contribute to this setting. I was skilled in the area of cosmetology and noticed many of the women were in need of haircuts or other simple processes. Most of these women had a fixed income and could mot spare the extra money to spend on themselves. All women want to feel good about themselves no matter what season in life they may be in. While I cut and styled the hair of these women, they shared with me personal experiences about their lives. I quickly realized that I was no better or worse than they. I came to the end of myself and began on the road of healing of my past. *God reveals himself to a humble heart.*

During this time I was doing a deep study on Exodus in the Bible. Exodus describes a series of God's calls and the responses of his people. God had heard the cry of his people and came to rescue them. God provided for their physical and spiritual needs with food and a place to worship, but he also judged their disobedience and unbelief. It's not easy to trade the comfortable security of the known for an uncertain future. We can be confident that God still hears the cries of his people. Just as he delivered the Israelites from their captors, he delivers us from sin, death, and evil. At times the Israelites became quarrelsome and discontent. Like the Israelites, we find it easy to complain and be dissatisfied. Christians still have struggles, but we should never allow difficulties and unpleasant circumstances to turn us away from trusting God. In the book of Exodus, God revealed his law to the Israelites. Through the law, they learned more about what God is like and how he expected his people to live. The law is still instructional for us, for it exposes our sin and shows us God's standard for living. Like the Israelites, we need both divine and human leadership to escape from the slavery of sin. God delivered us from the slavery of sin through his son Jesus Christ, who rescued us from sin by dying in our place. Although God is all-powerful and can do miracles, he normally leads us by wise leadership and team effort. God was teaching Israel the importance of choice and responsibility. When they obeyed the conditions of the law, he blessed them; if they forgot or disobeyed, he allowed calamities to come. God's moral law is valid today. We are often disorganized, sometimes rebellious, and sometimes victorious. God's person and Word are still our only guides. If you reflect his leadership, you will be effective in serving him. Exodus is the exciting story of *God's guidance and the determination of some to follow God wherever he leads.*

I personally had to deal with the *sin of unforgiveness.* Many things had happened in my past in which I had no control of. I had been harboring unforgiveness for the people who had inflicted pain or abuse against me. *Withholding forgiveness of others is a sin.* This particular sin had taken root in my life and I was completely unaware of it presence.

Luke 23:34: "Then Jesus said, Father, forgive them; for they know not what they do."

Jesus asked God to forgive the people who were putting him to death, and God answered that prayer by opening up the way to salvation even to Jesus's murderers. Because we are all sinners, we all played a part in putting Jesus to death. The Gospel—The Good News—is that God is gracious. He will forgive us and give us new life through his Son.

Matthew 6:14–15: "For if ye forgive men their trespasses, your heavenly Father will also forgive you: But if ye forgive not men their trespasses, neither will your Father forgive your trespasses."

Jesus gives a startling warning about forgiveness: if we refuse to forgive others, God will also refuse to forgive us. Why? Because when we don't forgive others, we are denying our common ground as sinners in need of God's forgiveness. God's forgiveness is based on our realizing what forgiveness means. God does not forgive us because we forgive others, but out of his great mercy.

Ephesians 4:32: "And be kind one to another, tenderhearted, forgiving one another, even as God for Christ's sake hath forgiven you."

As we come to understand God's mercy, we will want to be like him. Having received forgiveness, we will want to pass it on to others. Those who are unwilling to forgive have not become one with Christ, who was willing to forgive even those who crucified him.

Colossians 3:13: "Forbearing one another, and forgiving one another, if any man have a quarrel against any: even as Christ forgave you, so also do ye."

God places people into our lives who have already traveled through and overcome the area in life in which you are struggling. In my life, this person is Joyce Meyer. I was familiar with Joyce's personal testimony and her struggle in forgiving those who had abused her. Today, Joyce is a virtuous woman of God, who by God's good grace now has a worldwide ministry and a Christian television program, *Enjoying Everyday Life*.

Proverbs 31:10–31: "Who can find a virtuous woman? For her price is far above rubies. The heart of her husband doth safely trust in her, so that he shall have no need of spoil. She will do him good and no evil all the days of her life. She seeketh wool, and flax, and worketh willingly with her hands. She is like the merchants' ships; she bringeth her food from afar. She riseth also while it is yet night, and giveth meat to her household, and a portion to her maidens. She considereth a field, and buyeth it: with the fruit of her hands she planteth a vineyard. She girdeth her loins with strength, and strengtheneth her arms. She perceiveth, that her merchandise is good; her candle goth not out by night. She layeth her hands to the spindle, and her hands hold the distaff. She stretcheth out her hand to the poor; yea, she reacheth forth her hands to the needy, she is not afraid of the snow for her household; for all her household are clothed with scarlet. She maketh herself coverings of tapestry; her clothing is silk and purple. Her husband is known in the gates, when he sitteth among the elders of the land. She maketh fine linen and selleth it; and delivereth girdles unto the merchant. Strength and honour are her clothing; and she shall rejoice in time to come. She openeth her mouth with wisdom; and in her tongue is the law of kindness. She looketh well to the ways of her household, and eateth not the bread of idleness. Her children arise up, and call her blessed; her husband also, and he praiseth her. Many daughters have done virtuously, but thou excellest them all. Favour is deceitful, and beauty is vain: but a woman that feareth the lord, she shall be praised. Give her of the fruit of her hands; and let her own works praise her in the gates."

Effective leaders are rare. Joyce Meyer having distinguished herself as a woman of faith and courage has a strong spiritual influence on many, while maintaining the key to her success is her submission to God. Joyce is committed to obeying God, and when God spoke, Joyce listened and obeyed. God's work done in God's way will bring her success. Joyce's life reflects this truth. Strong leaders are led by God and her God given words have made a positive impact on my life. I became a partner with Joyce Meyers Ministries, watch "Enjoying Everyday Life," attend conferences, and have read many of her books. Receiving encouragement, edification, and uplifting advice from a woman who pressed in and never gave up through trials and tribulations. I became determined to succeed no matter what I would go through. A strong desire to become a virtuous woman of God myself, *I trusted the Lord to be with me every step of the way.*

Our strength to do God's work comes from trusting him. His promises reassure us of his love and that he will be there to guide us in the decisions and struggles we face. Faith begins with believing he can be trusted, and guidance from God for daily living can be found in his Word. By staying in touch with God, we will have the needed wisdom to meet the great challenges of everyday life. We must be ready to listen and move quickly. To love God means more than being enthusiastic about him. We must complete all the work he gives us and apply his instructions to every corner of our lives. Once we have his instructions, we must be diligent in carrying them out. Because of what God has done, we should have hope and follow him; because of what he expects, we should listen and obey; because of who he is, we should love him completely. God still calls his children to love him with all our heart, soul, and mind. Due to the head trauma I received at the time of the accident, I struggled with past memories, *so I asked God to renew my mind so I could have the life he offers me in Christ.*

Romans 12:1–2: "I beseech you therefore, brethren, by the mercies of God, that ye present your bodies a living sacrifice, holy, acceptable unto God, which is your reasonable service. And be not conformed to this world: but be ye transformed by the renewing of your mind, that ye may prove what is that good, and acceptable, and perfect, will of God."

God has a good, pleasing, and perfect plan for his children. He wants us to be new people with renewed minds, living in honor and obey him. Since he wants only the best for us, and since he gave his Son to make our new life possible, we should joyfully volunteer as living sacrifices for his service. Christians are called to "be not conformed to this world" with its behaviors and customs that are often selfish and corrupting. Many Christians wisely decide that much of the worldly behavior is off-limits to them. Our refusal to conform to this world's values however must go deeper than the level of behaviors and customs; it must be firmly founded in our minds: "Be ye transformed by the renewing of your mind." It is possible to avoid most worldly customs and still be proud, covetous, selfish, stubborn, and arrogant. Evaluating yourself by worldly standards of success and achievement can cause you to think too much about your worth in the eyes of others and miss your true value in God's eyes. The key to an honest and accurate evaluation of yourself is, *knowing the basis of your self-worth—your identity in Christ* (see Romans 8:5). Apart from him, we aren't capable of very much by eternal standards; in him, we are valuable and capable of worthy service.

During my time at the Healing House I received healing from my past and learned how to walk into my future with an expectation of victory. *God reveals himself to a trusting heart.*

The third and last life-changing experience I will discuss in detail is in the area of walking away from people or things that would hold you back from doing the will of God. This event happened approximately two years after my conversion and my personal decision to walk in obedience to the leading of the Holy Spirit.

Spiritual leaders of the church in which I had been an active member for the past ten years gathered together with me to discuss concerns about my recent behaviors. Everything they spoke of was in fact true, however they had no understanding of why. I highly respect the opinions of my spiritual leaders and listened to all the areas of their concerns. Considering my out of character behaviors and their feelings about how these behaviors were placing myself in unsafe situations, and how the behaviors were reflecting upon the church. The first thing discussed was about the noticeable decline in my area of giving in tithes. I explained, "I no longer own As We Grow Childcare, therefore no longer have the financial resources I had in the past. The entire truth is that the Lord had corrected me in this area of my life. When I did have control over my resources, I had not handled them properly. I had in fact given out of my abundance, now I give out of my lack, which is more than the biblical requirement."

Luke 12:11–21: "And when they bring you unto the synagogues, and powers, take no thought how or what thing ye shall answer, or what ye ought to say. And the company said unto him,

Master, speak to my brother, that he divide the inheritance with me. And he said unto him, Man, who made me a judge or divider over you? And he said unto them, Take heed, and beware of covetousness: for a man's life consisteth not in the abundance of the things which he possesseth. And he spake a parable unto them, saying, The ground of a certain rich man brought fourth plentifully: And he thought to within himself, saying, What shall I do, because I have no room where to bestow my fruits? And he said, This will I do: I will pull down my barns, and build greater; and there will I bestow all my fruits and my goods. And I will say to my Soul, thou hast much goods laid up for many years; take thine ease, eat, drink, and be merry. But God said unto him, Thou fool, this night thy soul shall be required of thee: then whose shall those things be, which thou hast provided? So is he that layeth up treasure for himself, and is not rich toward God."

I knew I could never dominate a religious dispute with the well-educated leaders of my church. Nevertheless, I was not left unprepared. Jesus promised that the Holy Spirit would supply the needed words. My relationship with the Lord was much more important to me than my livelihood. Jesus in me put his finger on this questioner's heart.

Realizing I was speaking the truth, and being aware of my education and experience in working with young children, the leaders took into consideration my situation and offered me a great opportunity within the church ministry. The children's ministry was in need of a director and supervisor. I politely declined the offer stating, "If God wanted me to continue in the area of children's ministry, he never would have required me to leave the position in which I was already settled and comfortable." They seemed offended at my response. The truth is, when you find yourself in a difficult situation in which you have no understanding. *You are to trust, relay and lean on every word of God.*

Psalms 37:3–6: "Trust in the Lord, and do good; so shalt thou dwell in the land, and verily thou shalt be fed. Delight thyself also in the Lord: and he shall give thee the desires of thine heart. Commit thy way unto the Lord; trust also in him; and he shall bring it to pass. And he shall bring forth thy righteousness as the light, and thy judgment as the noonday."

To commit ourselves to the Lord means entrusting everything we have and do to him. This includes our lives, families, jobs, possessions, etc., to his control and guidance. Believing that the Lord can care for us better than we can care for ourselves. We should be willing to wait patiently for him to work out what is best for us. To delight in someone means to experience great joy in his or her presence. This happens only when we know that person well. *Knowledge of God's great love for us will indeed give us delight.*

Psalms 125:1–2: "They that trust in the Lord shall be as mount Zion, which cannot be removed, but abideth forever. As the mountains are round about Jerusalem, so the Lord is round about his people from henceforth even forever."

The secret to consistency is to trust in God because he never changes. *God is completely reliable and will keep us steady.*

Another area of concern of my spiritual leaders was in the area of the company of people I now found myself in. They had been informed that I had opened the door of my home to a homeless man, and being a single woman myself, this was very inappropriate. I was told different members of the church had reported seeing my motorcycle located outside a well-known biker bar, and the pastor questioned my inappropriate behavior of leaving the church service prior to altar call.

I responded that Jesus himself entered into places and spoke to people that others felt were unworthy of their time. At this time in my life I did not feel comfortable enough to tell details of my past, so I simply stated, "*I am in process of receiving healing in my life. By the leading of the Holy Spirit, and to the very best of my ability, I walk in obedience to the will of God. I leave this church service early in order to attend another church service with a group of women who are going through the same process. As far as the homeless man is concerned, he has been a friend of mine for several years; completely harmless, and the truth is, he is adding more to my life than he is taking.*"

Matthew 9:9–13: "And as Jesus passed forth from thence, he saw a man, named Matthew, sitting at the receipt of custom: and he saith unto him, Follow me. And he arose, and followed him. And it came to pass, as Jesus sat at meat in the house, behold, many publicans and sinners came and sat down with him and his disciples. And the Pharisees saw it, they said unto his disciples, Why eateth your Master with publicans and sinners? But when Jesus heard that, he said unto them, They that be whole need not a physician, but they that are sick. But go ye and learn what that meaneth, I will have mercy, and not sacrifice: for I am not come to call the righteous, but sinners to repentance."

Matthew was a tax collector with a bad reputation for cheating people. When Jesus called Matthew to be one of his disciples, Matthew jumped up and followed, leaving a lucrative career. Sometimes the decision to follow Christ requires difficult or painful choices. Like Matthew, we must decide to leave behind those things that would keep us from following Christ. A few years earlier, I never would have opened my door to this friend, because I would have been concerned about what other people would say about me. Christians are not called to be people pleasers. When Jesus visited Matthew, he hurt his reputation. Matthew was cheating people, but Jesus found and changed him. We should not be afraid to reach out to people who are living in sin, because *God's message can change anyone.*

The homeless man and I had been friends for several years. He was a kind individual who would give the last penny in his pocket to help someone less fortunate. He was also an outspoken unbeliever in God. He often said, "I believe when it's over, we just become worm food." His favorite place to hang out was the well-known biker bar in which the members of my church had reported seeing my motorcycle at. If anyone of those people had dared to enter into the bar, they would have found me in the back area, sitting at a table with this man, reading the Bible, drinking a bottle of water and proudly flying my Christian back patch. The outlaw bikers highly respect Christian bikers and this patch clearly identifies whom I represent: *Our Lord and Savior, Jesus Christ.*

It was during one of my visits with this man that I discovered he had become homeless. I was delighted when he accepted my offer to stay in the back room of my house. I felt much safer with his presence in my home. He also cared for the lawn and my dog while I attended to the spiritual things in my life. In time this man was diagnosed with terminal throat cancer and moved into a nursing home to live out his last days. I continued to visit him as often as I could. On the last day I saw this man alive, he gave his life to Christ and asked the Lord for forgiveness of his sins. I had the privilege of speaking at his funeral and look forward to seeing him in eternity. *Allowing God to use your life for his glory; turning a lost soul toward the Kingdom of God by displaying Christ in you, is much more important than any sacrifice you may face in this world.*

Matthew 25:34–39: "Then shall the King say unto them on his right hand, Come, you blessed of my Father, inherit the Kingdom prepared for you from the foundation of the world: For I was an hungered, and you gave me meat: I was thirsty, and you gave me drink: I was a stranger, I and you took me in: Naked, and you clothed me: I was sick, and you visited me: I was in prison, and you came unto me, Then shall the righteous answer him, saying, Lord, when did we see you an hungered, and fed you? Or thirsty, and gave you drink? When did we see you a stranger, and took you in? Or naked, and clothed you? Or when did we see you sick, or in prison, and came unto you? And the King shall answer and say unto them, Verily I say unto you, In so much as you have done it unto one of the least of the brethren, you have done unto me."

I used this same scripture when the elderly couple picked me up from a street corner and took me safely back to my brother Steve. When I was in need God sent these angels to help me. I am honored to have had the same opportunity in my life to help another in need. *God's love, grace, and mercy is for everyone.*

During the meeting with my spiritual leaders, I remained steadfast to my convictions. At the conclusion many walked away stating, "If you do not change your behaviors and submit to the leadership of this church we will have no option but to ask you to leave!" To this day, I'm still amazed at my response, *"I am under the submission of the authority of God, in which you also have been called!"* I sat and thought about what had just accrued. I questioned my own sanity, thinking, "Is God truly speaking to me? My spiritual leaders are much more knowledgeable in the understanding of the word of God than I. Surely God would choose someone more educated than me! *I am so unworthy of such a blessing!"*

As the room cleared, one woman remained behind. Sitting down next to me, taking my hands into hers, she said, "Cindy, I believe what you are saying to be true." She then proceeded to share with me a very personal moment in her life, where she also had received the call from God to change her direction. She continued on saying, "Like you, many people doubted God could and would change me to be used for his glory. Like you, I knew it was God. Like you, I pressed in, determined that no matter what, I would never give up. I felt the need to reassure you in this journey you are on. You continue to follow the leading of the Holy Spirit, go where he tells you to go, do what he asks you to do and you will never be disappointed. As far as the leaders of this church are concerned, you allow me to talk with them, and know as surely as the Lord lives within me, you are always welcome here."

Standing steadfast to the convictions of my heart was very difficult. I felt like my world had just come to an end. Although I must admit, it felt real good to know that at least one person in the room that day believed. *God reveals himself to a servant's heart.*

Corinthians 10:11–14: "Now all things happed unto them for examples: and they are written for our admonition, upon whom the ends of the world are come. Wherefore let him that thinketh he standeth take heed lest he fall. There hath no temptation taken you but such as is common to man: but God is faithful, who will not suffer you to be tempted above that ye are able; but will with the temptation also make a way to escape, that ye may be able to bear it. Wherefore, my dearly beloved, flee from idolatry."

Is the world going to end soon? Even Jesus himself knows not when the end of the world would come—God alone knows (Mark 13:32). We have been living in the "last days" since Christ ascension. We are to be ready for Christ's return at any moment. *Anyone close to Christ will feel an urgency of spreading the Gospel.*

In a world filled with moral depravity and pressures take heed this encouragement in resisting temptations.

1. Temptations happen to everyone, so don't feel you've been singled out.

2. Others have resisted temptation and so can you.

3. Any temptation can be resisted, because God will help you resist it.

God helps you resist temptation by helping you recognize those people and situations that give you trouble. God helps you to run away from anything you know is wrong, and choose to do only what is right. Pray for God's help and seek other believers who love God and can offer help when you feel tempted. Running away from a tempting situation is your first step on the way to victory.

Trusting anything for what God alone provides is idolatry. Our modern idols are those symbols of power, pleasure, or prestige that we so highly regard, like paper money, plastic cards, or perhaps people in whom we have unhealthy high regard for.

Sometimes we may even see ourselves or feel like we deserve to be recognized and placed in a position of higher power. When you are in an area of leadership (everybody is a leader to somebody), self-pride can creep into an unaware soul. When we understand contemporary parallels to idolatry, to "flee from idolatry" becomes much more meaningful. I had been attending and was very active in the leadership of this church for ten years. I had grown in knowledge and understanding in spiritual warfare. I am very thankful for the spiritual guidance I received from leaders during that season of my life.

It was when I opened up the Bible and started studying the Word of God for myself, I discovered many misleading half-truths were being taught from the pulpit. I began praying and searching for a new church home. *God reveals himself to a faithful heart.*

Many people believe you should not ask God questions. They believe if you do, you are displaying weak faith and you are to just accept whatever comes your way. *God's Word says, "Ask, and it shall be given you!"* The answers to all life questions can be found *in the Word of God, the Bible.*

When I made the choice to open *what?*—*The Bible.*

How did I learn?—*I asked questions.*

Why did I *ask questions?*—To find answers to *what, when, how, where, why,* and *who!*

Where I found answers, to *what* I did not know, was *when* I made the time, and learned *how* to ask questions about *why* my life was so good, and *who* made it possible.

Everything in the *Bible,* points to *Jesus!*

I am a student of God's Word, and committed to receiving the full benefit of studying Scripture. I do not study just to increase knowledge, but I study the Word of God to increase my love for the divine Author!

God so loves you and me, that he gave his very best. His name is Jesus!

Today, I personally know Jesus!
Wow! Life is absolutely amazing!

Interrupting Satan's Plan by Releasing God's Power

Jeremiah 7:23: "But this thing commanded I them, saying, Obey my voice, and I will be your God and ye shall be my people: and walk ye in all the ways that I have commanded you, that it may be well unto you."

God had set up a system of sacrifices to encourage the people to obey him (see the book of Leviticus). He required the people to make these sacrifices, not because the sacrifices themselves pleased him, but because they caused the people to recognize their sin and refocus on living for God. They faithfully made the sacrifices but forgot the reason they were offering them, and thus they disobeyed God. Jeremiah reminded the people that acting out religious rituals was meaningless unless they were prepared to obey God in all areas of life.

This verse speaks volumes into my life. As a child, I was not taught the ways of the Lord. As a young adult, I started the search for happiness. True joy, peace, and love. It is easy for me to track my spiritual growth and journey because it started the day I gave birth to my daughter, Renee. That day I cried out to someone greater than myself, saying, "Give to me the ability to love unconditionally!" Today, I know God has given me the ability to love all people unconditionally, including myself, which was very difficult in the beginning. I had to learn many spiritual truths and how to apply them to my personal life. I had to be determined, diligent, and above all I had to learn, not to give up, no matter what the cost. Today, I consider myself a mature woman of God. Of course like all other Christians, I will continue to grow day by day until I bow before my Lord and Savior and see Jesus face to face. Today I look forward to that day. The Word of God says . . . He delights in giving his obedient children the desires of their heart. God has given me many desires of my heart. There are three I will speak of in this book. First on a personal level is my husband, Jay.

I had been working alone as a barber in a nice quite shop. I enjoyed the peaceful atmosphere and was able to study the Word of God in between haircuts. I suddenly became very busy with a large amount of flattops and questioned one of the new customers where he and all the others were coming from. He explained, "My normal barber had a heart attack and his business partner cannot handle all the customers on his own." After several weeks of many extra costumers, I thought to myself I need more work hours to care for all these people. The owner of the shop in which I was working would not give me more time so I decided to go to this other barber and tell him he needs to hire me and I will bring back to him his costumers. I had thought of all the things I should say in order to get hired and what rate of pay I required. Hopping on my motorcycle, I cruised around until I found The Barbershop. Around 4:00 p.m. on a Friday afternoon, I pulled into the parking lot, hopped off my bike and walked into the shop. Looking around I asked, "Hey, anybody in here named Jay?" A man cutting hair at the opposite side of the room looked at me and replied, "Yeah, it's me." Frozen in my steps, I gazed at this man; looked up toward heaven and whispered, "*Thank you, God!*"

I knew nothing about this man; all I knew was how I felt inside the moment I saw him. I knew, I was in the exact place God had purposed for me to be at this time in my life. I quickly pulled my thoughts together, walked up to Jay, shook his hand and said, "Hi, my name is Cindy, I'm your new barber and I will start work tomorrow." Jay then asked, "Can you cut a flattop?" "Yes," I replied. He then proceeded to tell me what hours he needed me to work and how much the pay would be. Both the hours and the pay were more than I would have requested, so I zipped my lip and simply nodded my head yes. We exchanged business cards and I left. That evening Jay called me and we talked of some concerns he had about hiring a woman. I reassured Jay everything would be all right and told him I needed to give a two-week notice at my current job before I can work full-time at his shop. I also requested a one-week vacation in-between the jobs, Jay agreed to all the terms; I was surprised and delighted at the same time. When I was settled in at this new job, Jay decided to take a vacation. Around two months later, we sat and talked for the first time.

Jay told me that at the exact moment I pulled up to the barber shop on my bike, the customer sitting in his chair had just stated, "Jay, you can't keep working like this, you really need to get some help." Jay acknowledged he did in fact need help and said, "He had heard of a blond barber biker chic that was in need of better working hours." He continued, "I swear at that moment, you turned in the driveway." The customer said, "Well there is your new blond barber biker chic right now." I laughed and said, "Maybe so." Jay continued to say, "I about fall over when you said what you said. I had never before mentioned that to anybody, until that day at that moment." Jay and I quickly became friends. The physical attraction was very strong and as we worked together, we discovered we had many things in common. After a few weeks Jay asked me, "What do you want in a man?"

I replied, "Two things, first we must agree on who is in control of our lives," pointing up, "and second he must have a motorcycle and love to ride." Jay purchased a new motorcycle that weekend and within that year, asked me to marry him. On Thanksgiving Day, three months after meeting Jay, I met his family. Jay has wonderful parents, a younger brother, aunts, uncles, and many cousins. One cousin who lived out of state and had not been to a family gathering in several years arrived and started collecting welcome back hugs from everyone. As he walked around the room everybody laughed and asked him the same question. "Do you remember me?" When he got to me, with a very serious look on my face, I also hug him and asked, "Do you remember me?" With a bewildered look, he stuttered, "I-I-I-don't think, I'm sorry, who-are you?" Everyone started laughing and I felt very welcomed into this amazing family unit. It was in that moment that I suddenly remembered that I also must have a personal family unit. At the end of day, after returning home, I sat down and started replaying the events of the night in my head. *"Do you remember me?"* kept playing over and over again in my mind. I prayed and asked God to give back to me my childhood memories. That night as I slept, I suddenly was awaken with a phone number in my head. I jumped up, got pen and paper, and wrote down 358-####. I was flooded with a variety of emotions. Excitement, expectation, but the strongest emotion was overwhelming fear. Why was I filled with fear? Why had nobody in my close family unit ever reach out to me? Was I such an awful person, that nobody cared about what had happened to me? Does anybody even remember me and know that I'm alive?

When I arrived at work I gave the number to Jay, asking him to call it and find out whom it belongs to. The person on the other end said, "Johnson Gas and Air." Motioning to Jay to hang up the phone, I told Jay, "That's my daddy's business!" As memories concerning Daddy started coming back I blurted out, "I love him, I miss him, it's been over twenty-five years since I last saw him. He-Is-Still-Alive, I must find him!"

Jay asked me many questions. When did I lose my memory? Why did I have no memory of my childhood? Why did God remove my memories? Why did God allow this to happen to me? What good could come out of it?

The motorcycle accident, (which was no accident, but purposed by the mighty hand of God, that much I was certain of) is *when* I lost my memory. I concentrated and answered many of my own thoughts and questions of why. *Now* I think I understand, at least in part.

I remembered prior to the accident, my spirit was grieved heavily for healing in the broken relationship between father and daughter. God allowed the accident, removed the childhood negative memory of abuse and abandonment of the past, so I could remain focused on the immediate positive changes that were to take place in my future. The first immediate change was the healing of my broken spirit and wounded soul. In becoming one with Jesus, I am *now* a healthy whole person. The second immediate change was learning how to teach my children the ways of the Lord. What an amazing blessing for a mother to know that all her children have made the right choice and are on the right path that leads to the foot of the cross. My children are *now* adults and in process of teaching my grandchildren the ways of the Lord. The third immediate change was learning how to wait and trust in God's timing for my life companion. God chose and put in order the things that brought Jay and I together. We are now married, growing together and serving the Lord. *Now I know* who the man is in my dreams and visions. He is *God's son, Jesus.* Because Jesus lives, I live! Because Jesus lives, I can face tomorrow! My tomorrows are just beginning! This fact is set in my mind, no one would ever again be placed before God! So the answer to *what good came* out of the temporary memory loss is, I now have a solid relationship with my Heavenly Father, and growing closer and stronger every day. God is *now* preparing the way back to my earthly father! *Thank you God*, all I could say was, *"Thank you God, for your love toward me."*

I called the 358-#### several times, identifying myself as Don Johnson's daughter and requesting a return phone call. The people answering the phone continued responding with the same remark, "I didn't know Don had a daughter." This confused me, so I asked God, "What's up with that?"

God gave to me a vision . . . I saw three hearts. The first heart was on fire, burning and falling downward in a never-ending pit. The second heart was black and behind bars. The third heart was pink and beating slow. I asked God to explain the vision to me. In my mind he revealed the meaning of the vision . . . the first heart represents the lost soul. The second heart represented the time frame of an individual's life when you are in bondage and captivity to sin. The third and pink heart represents the time frame of a clean and pure heart. My spiritual understanding of this explanation is that my daddy is saved, the slow beating heart, implies my daddy's time remaining here in this physical realm was short. A strong sense of urgency filled my spirit. No time to waste, I must find him now!

Together Jay and I prayed, asking the Lord to guide our footsteps. We then requested the service of a detective to locate my father and received all the information needed to make the connection. I was told Daddy had been attending a church for the past ten years. I was overjoyed at this great news. However, my joy was short-lived when the detective asked, "Does the name Kara mean anything to you?" Everyone present in the room saw my reaction at the mention of her name. I started shaking in uncontrollable fear. My facial expression changed from joy to disappointment as I stated, "That's his wife. Is she still alive?" In my heart I knew that no matter how I felt about Kara, I must respect Daddy and his marriage to her. In the eyes of God, Kara and Daddy are one and I would not see one without the other. I prayed continually for the Lord to open the door. *"Oh help me please God!"*

I remembered, Daddy had never been allowed to answer the phone. Kara filtered all calls, controlled all incoming, outgoing mail, and only gave her husband the information she felt appropriate. *Now*, I understand why I had not gotten a return phone call. I thought to myself, *"I will need supernatural intervention power to see Daddy again."* Out loud for all to hear I said, *"Because Jesus lives, all fear is gone."* Funny though, I didn't feel like all fear was gone. So I considered my words and added in a matter of fact voice, *"I can do all things through Christ which strengthens me."*

Christmas and my fiftieth birthday was fast approaching. Jay asked me to marry him. Of course I said yes. We decided on a six month engagement. During that time frame I continued trying to contact Daddy. I sent a certified letter to his home and told the people answering his business phone, "My name is Cindy, Don Johnson's only daughter. I would like for my daddy to have the privilege and honor of walking me down the aisle on my wedding day." Jay and I also drove our motorcycles by his resident. As we approached the house, I motioned for Jay to keep on moving. We pulled around the corner, stopped the bikes, and prayed. I told Jay, "I heard the Holy Spirit say, 'No good would come of this.'" "If no good will come of us stopping at this time, then we are to wait on God's instructions. God will tell me when the time is right, I must obey the Holy Spirit." Jay agreed with me and we *continued forward* in preparing our wedding day.

Prior to our wedding day we shared with each other all the details about our past. Jay was divorced with one grown daughter. I was a packaged deal, with one daughter, twin sons and six grandbabies. Although all of our children are now grown and starting families of their own, I knew that in the near future I would have to tell my children the painful truth of my past, which also affected them. I shared with Jay all the details I could remember of my abusive past and how God healed me from it. Jay stated, "I love you for who you are today, not for who you used to be, and I will love all of you, including your children and grandchildren." I added, "I also have a mentally ill brother I care for, and as we recently discovered together, a stepmother who hates me. Jay and I talked about our spiritual lives in detail. Who, when, where, what and how etc. The fact is, Jay and I had both made many wrong choices and suffered through the pain and consequences of those choices and we also now know how those choices affected the lives of so many other people.

I had asked God to give me someone I was equally yoked with. I expected someone with the same spiritual gifts. I was amazed and pleasantly surprised to discover that Jay and I have gifts opposite each other. I prayed, asking God for revelation on this matter. In my mind God placed understanding. Two people becoming one with different gifts and talents will be used for God's glory with twice as much impact. This will require husband and wife being bound together with God through prayer in all areas of life. Knowledge and understanding of a plan of action must be agreed upon by both and confirmed by God. Communication skills when operating together using different strengths will complement each other's spiritual gifts for God's glory. I thought in that revelation, "That seems simple enough—wonder why I had never thought of it before?" The answer, God's timing! *We must learn to wait on God's timing!* Jay and I would be tested and tried over and over again in this area. The good news is, that as children of God, *you cannot fail* a test of God. We will continue receiving test's until *we do pass. God is patient with us.*

Hebrews 13:1, 3–5: "Let brotherly love continue. Remember them that are in bonds, as bound with them; and them that suffer adversity, as being you also in the body. Marriage is honorable in all, and the bed undefiled: but whoremongers and adulterers God will judge. Let your conversation be without covetousness; and be content with such things as ye have: for he hath said, I will never leave or forsake."

Real love for others produces tangible actions. Hospitality to strangers, sympathy for those who are in prison ("in bonds"), those who have been mistreated, respect for one's marriage vows, and satisfaction with what you have. We are to have sympathy for those in bonds, especially for, but not limited to Christians imprisoned for their faith. Jesus said his true followers would visit those in prison as his representatives. (Matthew 25:36)

I never received a reply from Daddy for walking me down the aisle on my wedding day. Spiritually, I carried Daddy with me in my heart. On our wedding day, Jay's daughter Corey, my daughter Renee, and sister Michelle walked into the church first. Followed by my twin sons, Ron and Stan proudly escorting me down the aisle and giving me to my husband. Physically this was something we all needed to experience. For years to the best of my ability, I had been both mother and father to my children. My children needed to release themselves out from under my physical care, and I needed to let go and allow God's plan to unfold in their lives. Both Jay and I had worked long hard hours to support our children's needs and provide a full and exciting life. We both had experienced owning many way cool things including our own business, cool cars, and a beautiful home, yet we were both very lonely people. The time to move forward into a new season in life was appropriate and right. Joining together as husband and wife is pleasing in the Lords sight and I'm sure *God smiled upon us.*

Together with prayer, we made the decision to sell our large independent homes and live in a small but very comfortable space. In making this decision, God provides more than enough income to live very exciting lives. We travel often and see all the beautiful things God created. Our work demand is minimal so our time is freed up. We are able to attend spiritual growth classes, and we are very active in the ministry of our church. We agree that God is in control of all areas of our lives. As we continue to grow stronger spiritually, all else is falling in place. We have now been married several years. *Our lives are filled with joy and a peace that surpasses understanding.*

I had a dream: I saw myself juggling several very important different items. If one of the items fell, I would stoop down, pick it up, and begin juggling again. I was so focused on keeping the items in sequence that *I stood completely still.* I heard the Lord speak, "This is not the way I would have you to be; let me show you." I saw Jesus standing on a platform calling for me to walk forward. On the opposite side of the room, I saw myself also on a platform. In-between the platforms is a long tightrope. Underneath and all around was a safety net. Jesus said, "Plant your feet firmly on the Word of God, stretch your arms as far as the east is from the west, hold your head high, forget what lies behind and press forward to what lies ahead." I obeyed the Lord, took a step, but stumbled and fell. I bounced a couple of times in the safety net and lie on my back, looking up. "Stay in the net, climb the ladder, and *try again.*" I heard the Lord say. Again I obeyed. *I got repositioned to try again.* This time I opened my mouth and spoke out promises of the Lord. In time, I made it into the Lords arms. As Jesus embraced me, he said, "Now my child, I want you to walk back out on the tightrope, I want you to sing, dance and speak truth to my people." I responded, "Yes Lord, I will *do all* you ask of me," and woke up.

Acts 2:17–18: "And it shall come to pass in the last days, saith God, I will pour out of my Spirit upon all flesh: and your sons and your daughters shall prophesy, and your young men shall see visions, and your old men shall dream dreams: And on my servants and on my handmaidens I will pour out in those days of my Spirit; and they shall prophesy."

The "last days" include all the days between Christ's first and second comings and is another way of saying "from now on." Acts 2:17–18 was spoken by one of Jesus's first disciples. Peter had been an unstable leader during Jesus's ministry, letting his bravado be his downfall, even denying that he knew Jesus (John 18:15–18, 25–27). But Christ had forgiven and restored him. This was a new Peter, humble but bold. His confidence came from the Holy Spirit, who made him a powerful and dynamic speaker.

Have you ever felt as if you've made such bad mistakes that God could never forgive and use you? No matter what sins you have committed, God promises to forgive them and make you useful for his Kingdom. Allow him to forgive you and use you effectively to serve him. I dared to say, use my life Lord for your glory! I dared to say, my life is not my own, I am willing to go, please send me Lord! God knows my heart condition and knows I was sincere with my words. My life has become an amazing journey! I challenge you to say the same thing.

The second desire of my heart I would like to share about is my local church. God has established three major institutions on earth: the family, civil government, and the local church. All three provide something no other organization is able to give. They are unique because God ordained each one with leadership, blessings, and accountability. The local church has been commissioned by God to carry out his purpose in reaching the lost and perfecting the saved. The local church is a spiritual authority in your life, and God's plan for your life can be fulfilled when connected to right local church.

At the time I met my husband, I had been actively searching for a new church. I had been a believer for several years serving the Lord by the leading of the Holy Spirit. My husband had also been a believer for several years, and was beginning to understand the tugging in his heart to be that of the Holy Spirit. *Now together, we continued*; we visited several different churches. Many of the churches seemed comfortable to him, I however needed a church that offered a much deeper level of teaching. I was specifically looking for a church that would educate, equip, and edify us for the work of the ministry. A church that would provide spiritual leadership and prepare us to *live for God and fulfill our individual role in the Great Commission.*

Your role in the local church is vital. You should grow through three broad general stages.

1. You are to be perfected as a saint. (A time to observe and learn.) Your first priority should be to submit to the teaching of the word of God and the leadership of the church to learn to be the person God wants you to be. Even if you have some maturity in the Lord and in the Bible, you should understand that every local church is unique. You cannot serve effectively unless you follow leadership and prove yourself based on the particular ministry of the local church.

2. You are to do the work of the ministry. (A time to participate.) In time, you should naturally grow to the point where you can begin to serve God by taking on some basic functions through the ministries that are already established in your church.

3. You are to edify the body of Christ. (A time to lead.) As your spiritual growth continues, you should reach the point where you can begin to minister to others in the same way others have ministered to you.

Ephesians 4:11–16: "And he gave some, apostles; and some, prophets; and some, evangelists; and some, pastors and teachers; For the perfecting of the saints, for the work of the ministry, for the edifying of the body of Christ: Till we all come in the unity of the faith, and of the knowledge of the Son of God, unto a perfect man, unto the measure of the stature of the fullness of Christ: That we henceforth be no more children, tossed to and fro, and carried about with every wind of doctrine, by the sleight of men, and cunning craftiness, whereby they lie in wait to deceive; But speaking the truth in love, may grow up into him in all things, which is the head, even Christ: From whom the whole body fitly joined together and compacted by that which every joint supplieth, according to the effectual working in the measure of every part, maketh increase of the body unto the edifying of itself in love."

Jay and I prayed, asking God for wisdom in locating the right church for us.

James 1:5: "If any of you lack wisdom. Let him ask of God, that giveth to all men liberally, and upbraideth not; and it shall be given him."

When James speaks of wisdom, he means practical discernment. Wisdom begins with respect for God, leads to right living, and results in increased ability to tell right from wrong. God is willing to give us this wisdom, but we will be unable to receive it if our goals are self-centered instead of God-centered. To learn God's will, we need to read God's Word and ask him to show us how to obey it. Then we must do what he tells us.

In time we found the church that is a great fit for us. We continue to grow spiritually and are actively serving in the Motorcycle Ministry. Once a month I have the opportunity to speak at a home for the elderly. This is developing my skills in public speaking and I thank God for this amazing opportunity as *I share about His unconditional love toward all people.*

1 Corinthians 8:1–3: "We know that we all possess knowledge. Knowledge puffs up, but love builds up. The man who thinks he knows something does not yet know as he ought to know. But the man who loves God is known by God."

Love is more important than knowledge. Knowledge makes us look good and feel important, but one can easily develop an arrogant, know-it-all attitude. Many people with strong opinions are unwilling to listen and learn from God and others. We can obtain God's knowledge only by loving him (See James 3:17, 18).

Ephesians 6: 13–20: "Wherefore take unto you the whole armor of God, that ye may be able to stand in the evil day, and having done all, to stand. Stand therefore, having your loins girt about with truth, and having on the breastplate of righteousness; And your feet shod with the preparation of the gospel of peace; Above all, taking the shield of faith, wherewith ye shall be able to quench all the fiery darts of the wicked. And the helmet of salvation, and the sword of the Spirit, which is the Word of God: Praying always with all prayer and supplication in the Spirit, and watching thereunto with all perseverance and supplication for all the saints; And for me, that utterance may be given unto me, that I may open my mouth boldly, to make known the gospel, For which I am an ambassador in bonds: that therein I may speak boldly, as I ought to speak."

In the life of a Christian, we battle against "principalities and powers" (the powerful evil forces of fallen angels headed by Satan who is a vicious fighter (see 1 Peter 5:8). Those who are not "flesh and blood" are demons over whom Satan has control. They are not mere fantasies—they are very real. We face a powerful army whose goal is to defeat Christ's church. When we believe in Christ and join his church, these beings become our enemies, and they try every device to turn us away from Christ and back to sin. To withstand their attacks, we must depend on God's strength and use every piece of his armor. The whole body needs to be armed. As you do battle against "the rulers of the darkness of this world," fight in the strength of the church, whose power comes from the Holy Spirit. Although we are assured of victory, we must engage in the struggle until Christ comes, because Satan is constantly battling against all who are on the Lord's side. We need supernatural power to defeat Satan, and God provided that in his Holy Spirit within us and his armor surrounding us.

How can anyone pray all the time? One way to pray constantly is to make quick, brief prayers your habitual response to every situation you meet throughout the day. Another way is to order your life around God's desires and teachings so that your life becomes a prayer. You do not have to isolate yourself from other people and from daily work in order to pray constantly. You can make your life a prayer while living in a world that needs God's powerful influence. If you feel discouraged, remember Jesus's words to Peter: "Upon this rock I will build my church; and the gates of hell shall not prevail against it."

The third desire of my heart and promise of the Lord I would like to share with you is the reconciliation between my physical father, Don Johnson, and myself. The Lord had opened up my memory, and provided a phone number. Although several attempts to contact Daddy prior to my wedding day had been made, all had failed. After returning home from our honeymoon, my husband encouraged me to try again.

Although I am the same person, I now have a different last name and using God given wisdom, I chose not to identify myself as Don's daughter. I prayed, picked up the phone and dialed 358-####. I identified myself to the receiver as Cindy (new married name), looking for Don Johnson. "Please have him return my call as soon as possible," I stated, and hung up the phone. Within one minute the phone rang, I looked at the caller ID, saw it was from 358-####, and picked up the receiver. "Hello," I said and waited for a response. Although the caller never identified herself, I immediately recognized the voice on the other end to be that of Kara. "Is this Cindy (new married name)?" she asked. "Yes," I replied and continued, "I would like to speak to my father please." Kara then said words that I will never forget, "You are too late, your father is already dead!" and hung up the phone. I also hung up the phone, told my husband what she said and frankly stated, "She has always lied to me and I will not believe her this day. Besides God has already told me that my father lives!" *God keeps us strong and steady.*

I received a vision from God: I saw the Lord standing on the far side of a bridge, calling for me to come to him. The bridge crossed over very troubled water. I started to cross. At the halfway point, I saw the Lord raise his hand to stop me, tilting his head and moving his eyes to the right; directing me to the edge of the bridge. I moved to the edge and looked over. I heard the Lord ask, *"Do you trust me?"* I responded, "Yes, Lord, I do trust you!" "If you trust me, jump into the water!" said the Lord. Knowing my faith was being tested I jumped feet first into the fast moving troubled water. Instantly I was pulled downward by the undercurrent. Struggling to get my head up for air, I battled the strong current while being pulled under the bridge. I felt my body go limp, lost all strength and *gave up the struggle for control* over the situation. Drifting downward, reaching upward with my weak hand, I suddenly felt the strong arm of the Lord reach through the current and take hold of my arm. With one intense movement he lifted me from the water and placed me standing upright on top the bridge. *The Lord smiled at me and together we continued across the bridge.*

I understood the interpretation of this vision to mean that if I was to succeed I must totally trust and immediately obey God. The Jesus in me would be returning back home to my daddy and my past. *This was not to be my victory but God's. And the glory belongs to him.*

With the information provided by the detective, by phone, I made contact with my grandfather (Kara's stepfather). I remembered, at the time Daddy married Kara, this elderly couple accepted and welcomed both Steve and me into the family with love. I was around twelve years old the last time I had seen my grandparents. Nearly forty years had passed. I prayed, dialed the number, and immediately recognized the voice on the other end to be that of grandfather. I boldly stated, "Grandpa, this is Cindy, do you remember me?"

"Why yes, darling, I remember you!" He replied and continued, "Grandmother and I have been praying for you and Steve for years. We know what happened to you guys during your childhood, please forgive us for not doing more about it." I assured grandfather that he and grandmother had done more than they could ever imagine while here in this physical realm. They had tapped into the most powerful resource available to humankind, *they prayed!* I continued saying, "God has already forgiven you for not doing more and I could not add anything to what God has already done." We talked for hours concerning that had taken place in our lives. I was told that after the abandonment of Steve and me, they disconnected from Don and Kara for several years and later decided to return because of their grandson, Bobby.

Grandmother, Uncle Jerry, and Uncle Dale passed away a few years ago. Including himself, they had talked with my dad concerning finding Steve and me. Grandfather said that after my father started attending church he purchased a cell phone, never told Kara, and has ever since been waiting for a call from us. Of course I was unaware of what my father had done until this conversation but it felt good knowing that God had placed Steve and me on his mind. Grandfather provided me with the cell phone number of Daddy and the phone numbers to many aunts, uncles, and cousins that are all grown up now with families of their own. I thanked grandfather for his honesty, told him I looked forward to seeing him again soon and finished the conversation with, *"God is on my side, so victory is guaranteed!"*

I then tried Daddy's cell phone numerous times with no success. I made contact with the other people grandfather had provided numbers for and received similar responses. All were happy to hear Steve and I were well and most had separated themselves from the family due to Kara's behaviors. When I asked for their opinion concerning the welfare of my little brother, most said he was much like his mother (I will just leave it at that). All these people are related to Kara in some way, even if only thru marriage. As spoken about in chapter 1, I only had contact with Daddy's relatives during the first five years of my life, and I do not remember any of them. With the information provided by my cousins it was clear to me that Kara had not stopped at separating Steve and me from Dad but had continued with this course of division until the entire family unit had been split. I know that this next statement will sound selfish and perhaps even unchristian, but remember I am only human. It felt good knowing I was not the only one that experienced the painfulness of being separated from Daddy's life and feeling unwelcomed, unwanted, and unloved in Kara's presence.

Job 4:8, 9: "Even as I have seen, they that plow iniquity, and sow wickedness, reap the same. By the blast of God they perish, and by the breath of his nostrils are they consumed."

These words were spoken by Eliphaz, a close personal friend of Job's. All material recorded and quoted in the Bible is there by God's choice. Some is there as a record of what people said and did, but not as an example to follow. The sins, the defeats, the evil thoughts and misconceptions about God are all part of God's divinely inspired Word, but that does not mean we are to follow these wrong examples just because they are in the Bible. The Bible gives us teachings and examples of *what we should do* as well as what *we should not do*. Part of what Eliphaz said is true, and part is false. *It is true* that those who promote sin and trouble will eventually be punished: *it is false* that anyone who is good and innocent will never suffer. Eliphaz comments are an example of what we should try to avoid—*making false assumptions* about others based on our own experiences. God's Word says, it is not for us to know the times nor seasons. As God's obedient children, we must accept his timetable, even when we do not understand it. I know that the God I worship has an unconditional love for all he has created. God has a plan and purpose for each and every one of his creatures and as long as a person is experiencing life in this physical realm, *there is hope for change.*

The first physical contact I made with family members was my little brother Bobby and his family. As already spoken of in previous pages, this contact was made at the church in which Daddy is a member. After the church service, we went to lunch together and talked. Bobby did most of the talking—I listened carefully to every word spoken. Bobby said he also had a difficult time growing up in a non-Christian home. Explaining that he had a rough season in his life when he became addicted to drugs. His words, "I was a junkie, I thank God for my wife Ann, who stood by me and encouraged me through the healing process." When he finished talking, I asked, "How are you today and how is your relationship with our parents? He replied, "I've been clean for several years and my relationship with Mom and Dad is good." I told Bobby of my accident, the coma, and my memory loss. This was a true fact, however Bobby did not ask, and I avoided informing him, that my memory had been fully restored by God.

Because the stories Bobby had heard and believed to be true about Steve and me were in fact half-truths twisted with downright lies, I said, "Bobby there always are two sides to every story and the truth is usually found in the middle." I found it interesting, that Bobby's twelve-year-old son made this statement. "Hey, Dad, what's up? I've been a member of this family all my life, yet I never knew you had a sister and brother." Bobby responded, "You are just a child, you didn't need to know. There are lots of things that are spoken of only between the adults." If Bobby had listened to his own words, Bobby would have been able to hear more clearly the truth for himself. (We were only children when the family had been split apart with Bobby being the youngest.) When spiritual beings are born again, we go thru the same process as we did in the physical. We are infants unable to care for ourselves. As we grow we trust the authority over us to guide us thru the process until we reach maturity.

Bobby said he would talk with his mother and dad and encourage them to allow me to return home. I thought to myself, I wish I could be a fly on the wall when that conversation takes place, seeing how Kara already knew I was trying to make contact and told me Daddy was dead. Of course I did not tell Bobby this and would *continue to trust God to unfold his plans in his time.* I did tell Bobby, "I will wait for your phone call."

I later discovered, by another person who was present at the time of this conversation with my stepmother what was said. I was told that when Bobby told his mother and dad that I found him at the church they attend, Kara became very upset and insisted that Dad find another church to go to. Daddy opposed her. Remember, *unbeknown to Kara,* Daddy had purchased a cell phone and was waiting on God to return Steve and me back to him. *Unbeknown to Kara,* Daddy was listening to the guiding of the Holy Spirit in his life. The Word of God says, a wise woman will pray for the desires of her husband's heart. How sad, if you are married, and do not know the desires of your companion's heart. Only when your hearts become one with God can true love be experienced as God intended. *God brings man and woman together to become one with him.*

A few days passed, the phone rang displaying the number 358-####. I thanked God for his strength in this moment, picked up the receiver and said, "Hello." I recognized the responding voice to be that of Kara. She said, "Cindy, this is your mom, (not) I've been praying for you (not). Bobby told me of your accident, *how much do you remember?*" I replied, "I remember enough." Kara continued, "Dad and I would like to see you, what time works for you?" Kara and I agreed to meet at Red Lobster for dinner and hung up the phone.

I went to my normal place of prayer, a quite spot in my bedroom and had a long conversation with God. In the beginning I did all the talking, I stated, "Mom! This-woman-is-not-my-mom. I have a mom! As a matter of fact, I have been blessed with two moms. My birth mother Ellen, and Pat, my husband's mother. Both my moms *accept and love me* for who I am today. Surely God, you don't expect me to call Kara—Mom! I have no respect for this woman. She has hurt me, wounded, and abused me, and the scars of her abuse run deep."

In my mind, the Lord placed this thought *"forgive her."* Out loud I screamed the thought, *"Forgive her!"* and continued on with this one-sided conversation. *"I can't! There is no way humanly possible I can forgive her. Do you realize what you are asking me to do?"* I became silent and clearly heard and followed the instructions of the Holy Spirit—the Spirit said, "Reposition thyself." I lifted my head up from my hands and with my eyes I scanned the room. In the *darkness* my eyes fall upon a chair located in the corner of the room, I repositioned myself to that location and waited for more instructions. (In my life, this unforgiveness toward Kara was the *darkness* hidden in the deepest *corner* of my heart. A place of bondage that only God could free me from.) "Lift your arms to me and lose your tongue," said the Spirit. I obeyed. Suddenly I felt a rushing flowing over and through me, like I was sitting under a powerful waterfall. I started speaking words that I had no understanding of. (This had happened only one other time in my life—when I was lifted up from the water during baptism.) Uncontrollable tears were rolling down my cheeks and falling on the floor. I kept my eyes closed during this process, however, I sensed the overhead light in the bedroom coming on and the presence of someone else enter in the room and leave again. When the Holy Spirit accomplished the washing of my inner self, I felt very weak and at the exact same time total refreshed. Upon wobbly legs I stood and headed in the direction of the bathroom to wash my face. At the top of the stairs I saw my husband and fell into his arms. Jay caught, balanced me, and asked what had happened. I told him and asked, "Did you turn on the light, come in the room, and leave again?" "Yes," he said and continued, "you disappeared for a long time so I came to find you." Jay paused for a moment then concluded, "Whatever was happening back in that corner I figured was between you and God, so I left." "It seemed like only a moment to me, how long was I gone?" I asked. "About an hour," Jay replied.

Smiling at me, he said, "Wait till you see your face." I went to the bathroom, looked at myself in the mirror and what a mess, sums it all up. I reapplied my make-up three times that day and cried it back off every time. These were not tears of sorrow, but joy. Throughout the remainder of the day encouraging scripture continued to fill my mind. I laughed, sang praises, danced, and over and over again said, *"I love you God and I love my life."*

Acts 2:2, 4: "And suddenly there came a sound from heaven as of a rushing mighty wind, and it filled the house where they were sitting. And they were filled with the Holy Ghost, and began to speak with other tongues, as the Spirit gave them utterance."

1 Corinthians 14:2: "For he that speaketh in an unknown tongue speaketh not unto men, but unto God: for no man understandeth him; howbeit in the spirit he speaketh mysteries."

Speaking in tongues is a legitimate gift of the Holy Spirit. Sometimes God will make his presence known to his children in a spectacular way—roaring wind, fire, powerful waterfalls, or God's message may come in a "still small voice." God may use a dramatic method to work in your life, or he may speak in gentle whispers. Few topics have caused division like speaking in tongues. Many believe God never uses the gift of tongues today. Many others believe God always gives the gift of tongues to every true believer. As I said before, I believe we are wise to avoid words like never and always when speaking on the power of God. How God chooses to show his presence and power is God's choice and we should not question it. *We are told to love each other, not judge one another.*

Jay and I purposely arrived at Red Lobster one hour before the meeting time agreed upon so we could pray prior to seeing Daddy and Kara. I held in my hands the Bible and photo albums containing pictures of our children and special events that had taken place over the past thirty years. You might think that after receiving the empowering of the Holy Spirit a few hours earlier, I would have it altogether. Wrong, I was scared out of my mind! I needed guidance so Jay and I prayed.

Psalms 25:1–8: "Unto Thee, O Lord, do I lift up my soul. O my God, I trust in thee; let me not be ashamed, let not mine enemies triumph over me. Yea, let none that wait on thee be ashamed; let them be ashamed that transgress without cause. Show me thy ways, O Lord; teach me thy paths. Lead me in thy truth, and teach me: for thou art the God of my salvation; on thee do I wait all day. Remember, O Lord, thy tender mercies and thy loving kindness; for they have been ever of old. Remember not the sins of my youth, nor my transgressions: according to thy mercy remember thou me for thy goodness' sake, O Lord. Good and upright is the Lord: therefore will he teach sinners in the way."

Psalms is a great book to find prayer for any situation. This great collection of songs and prayers expresses the heart and soul of humanity. In them, the whole range of human experiences is expressed. The writers honestly pour out their true feelings, reflecting a dynamic, powerful, and life-changing friendship with God. The psalmists confess their sins, express their doubts and fears, ask God for help in times of trouble, and praise and worship him. In psalms, you will hear believers crying out to God from the depths of despair, and you will hear them singing to him in the heights of celebration. You will always hear honesty in the sharing of true feelings with God. *Honesty will guide you into a deep and genuine relationship with God.*

I needed direction and guidance. Despite sinning when I was younger, I now have a close relationship with God because I have been forgiven. Today I know that God is unlimited, is all conquering, and has unrestrained authority over all creation and over each individual. I know God will triumph—*what I desire is to be a good representative for God in faith.*

Daddy, Kara, and to my delight Grandfather arrived and I introduced Jay. Daddy appeared healthy for his age, now in his seventies. Kara, now in her sixties, was wheelchair bound. The men sat at one side of the table, started talking and laughing. I sat next to Kara, opened the photo album, started flipping thru the pages and talked about my children and grandchildren. Kara showed some interest but preferred to talk about her medical conditions. In a short amount of time we came to a point where we had no more in common and sat silently looking at each other. I then jumped up, grabbed the album and boldly said, "I'm going to show Daddy." Yes, (I call him Daddy!) something Kara had forbid me to do. And in case you are wondering, yes (I called Kara, Mom). *God asked me to cover myself in humility, and in obedience to God, I obeyed.*

Kara told me, "Your father has dementia and will not remember you and he does not care about your family." "I'm going to show him anyway," I said, as I walked away from Kara. Opening the album before my father, I looked him square in the face and stated, "You know who I am, don't you, Daddy?" "Yes, of course I do!" "I knew you did!" Daddy, Grandpa, Jay, and I looked and laughed at the pictures for a long time. Before the evening was over we agreed on a date, place and time where they could *meet Renee, Stan, and Ron and their children (grandchildren).*

The second meeting took place in a private room with a full banquet provided. All immediate family members were present. All talked, laughed, and shared stories. It was during this time I discovered that Daddy did in fact have early onset dementia and was struggling with some memory loss. (I can certainly relate to the frustration of memory loss issues.) I also asked about the fact that my daddy now has only one eye and is in fact half blind. I was told he lost his eye in a working related accident. I understood this true fact—that during this season of their elderly lives, Daddy and Kara depend on each other and do in fact, need each other. Daddy bounced all around the room interacting with all his grandchildren and great-grandchildren. It felt good inside to see Daddy reaching out and connecting with his family. Kara also tried to interact, but often was left by herself, sitting in her wheelchair, watching what was taking place in the lives of everyone else. I could not help but notice how uncomfortable and out of place she appeared. As I looked in her direction this amazing thing took place inside of me, *I was filled with compassion toward her.*

John 5:5–8: "And a certain man was there, which had an infirmity thirty and eight years. When Jesus saw him lie, and knew that he had been now a long time in that case, he saith unto him, Wilt thou be made whole? The impotent man answered him, Sir, I have no man, when the water is troubled, to put me into the pool: but while I am coming, another steppeth down before me. Jesus saith unto him, Rise, take up thy bed, and walk."

John 5:1–15: "Is a short story about "Jesus heals a lame man by the pool" After thirty-eight years, this man's problem had become a way of life. No one ever helped him. He had no hope of ever being healed and no desire to help himself. His situation looked hopeless. But no matter how trapped you feel in your infirmities, God can minister to your deepest needs. Don't let a problem or hardship cause you to lose hope. God may have special work for you to do in spite of your condition, or even because of it. Many have ministered to hurting people because they have triumphed over their own hurts."

As you read this entire short passage, you will discover how Jesus healed this lame man. Yes, Jesus had compassion for his condition, but Jesus did not put the lame man into the pool. Instead Jesus said, "Arise, take up thy bed, and walk." In other words, Jesus said, "Get up, do your part, and you will be healed." Are you ready for change? Do you want to get well? *If you want a breakthrough, you must learn to go through!*

A great miracle took place in this short story. A lame man was healed and could now walk. But he needed even a greater miracle— to have his sins forgiven. The man was delighted to be physically healed, but *he had to turn from his sins and seek God's forgiveness* to be spiritually healed. Don't neglect his gracious offer. *God's forgiveness is the greatest gift you will ever receive.*

Psalms 147:3: "He healeth the broken in heart, and bindeth up their wounds."

God is the hope and help of the needy.

Jesus affirms his concern for the poor and afflicted in Luke 4:18–21, 7:21–23. He does not separate the physical from the spiritual needs of people, but attends to both. While God is the hope of the needy, we are his instruments to help here on earth.

After the family gathering I called weekly requesting another visit with my father. Kara, of course, always answered the phone and always told me Daddy was busy or not at home. I would try to have a conversation with Kara but we had absolutely nothing in common but Dad, so not much was said. Kara *did not know that I already knew* how to get to their home but she still made it clear to me that I was not to visit without her approval first. Months passed. April is Daddy's birthday, so I mail a birthday card. May is Mother's Day and I mailed Kara a card. Father's Day was fast approaching so I purchased Daddy a Father's Day card, made contact with Kara and requested a time of visitation so I could personally hand it to him. Kara said, "Your father is going on a fishing trip with Bobby and will be gone for three weeks so you may as well not call again until then." Because *I was aware* of her deceiving behaviors, I doubted she was speaking truth and replied, "*I will still call and talk with you.*" "So I am important after all," she remarked. "You are married to my father, you have been a part of my life and above all else you are *very important to Jesus,*" I responded. I believe those words caught Kara completely off guard—she had no response of her own. *The truth is, there is power in the name of Jesus,* at the mention of his name—walls come down.

No matter how you may feel about an offensive person whenever you remind them of God's love the conversation will end well. I told Jay what Kara said and we both agreed she was lying to me about the fishing trip. On Father's Day, Jay encouraged me to *try calling again.* Kara answered and told me Dad was not there. After hanging up and feeling defeated I broke down and started crying. Comforting me, Jay said, "I bet your dad's sitting right next to her!" I agreed with my husband and said, "*Daddy must reach out to me. There is no more I can do.*" Just then the phone rang. It was Kara. She told me, "*Your father wants to speak to you.*" And Daddy got on the phone.

I said, "Happy Father's Day, Daddy, I've miss you, it's been months since I've seen you. What have you been doing?" He replied, "I miss you too, sweetheart, why haven't you guys come over?" *In my heart I knew God would be pleased if I would maintain a peaceful attitude.*

Maintaining a peaceful attitude would require being humble and honest at the same time. I responded to Daddy's question stating, "I was told you have been working hard and you are never around." Grabbing ahold of the opportunity to put out some information without saying anything negative, therefore remaining peaceful, I choose my words carefully and continued, "I was told you are going on a fishing trip with Bobby for three weeks." Not allowing Daddy anytime to respond I quickly added, "Jay and I love fresh fish, sure hope you bring home some fish for Jay and me." *Now I paused and waited.* Daddy said, "Who told you that? I'm not going fishing!" "Why it was your wife of course that told me this." Again I continued speaking fast, "By the way, Daddy, did you get your Father's Day card?" "No," he replied. Thinking quick I then asked, "Did you get your birthday card?" "No," he replied." "O' really, well I mailed them to you. *I spent a lot of time picking out just the right ones with just the right words, just for you.* I know I sent them to the right address. You should have gotten them both weeks ago. I wonder what could have happened to them. Maybe your wife got them and forgot to give them to you. Maybe you should ask her, what happened to your cards!" Suddenly, very loudly I heard Daddy yell, "*Kara*, where is my birthday card?" In the background I heard her respond, "It's not your birthday, it's Father's Day." Knowing she was trying to confuse him by avoiding the question with a statement and also knowing Daddy could still hear me I quickly said, "I mailed you both cards, Daddy—a birthday card and a Father's Day card. *I remembered both those important dates, Daddy, because you are very important to me.* No matter what anyone else may tell you remember this—I love you and I want to see you again. Allow Jay and I to take you and Mom out for dinner. Mother and Father's Day, we'll treat. What's your favorite steak house? Let's set that date right now. *You decide!*" Daddy and I agreed on a date, place, and time for our next meeting. Before hanging up the phone, I gently and lovingly said, "*See you soon, Daddy.*"

Matthew 5:3–9: "Blessed are the poor in spirit: for theirs is the kingdom of heaven. Blessed are they that mourn: for they shall be comforted. Blessed are they which do hunger and thirst after righteousness: for they shall be filled. Blessed are the merciful: for they shall obtain mercy. Blessed are the pure in heart: for they shall see God. Blessed are the peacemakers: for they shall be called children of God."

In the Kingdom of heaven, wealth and power and authority are unimportant. Kingdom people seek different blessings and benefits, and they have different attitudes. Are your attitudes a carbon copy of the world's selfishness, pride, and lust for power, or do they reflect the humility and self-sacrifice of Jesus, your King. Being "blessed" by God means the experience of hope and joy, independent of outward circumstances. God's way of living usually contradicts the world's. If you want to live for God you must be ready to say and do what seems strange to the world. You must be willing to give when others take, to love when others hate, to help when others abuse. By giving up your own rights in order to serve others, *you will one day receive everything God has in store for you.*

Before the date of the next meeting arrived, I received a phone call from Kara. Sobbing and with broken sentences she managed to inform me of news concerning Dad. Daddy had received the diagnosis of terminal cancer and had been given six months to get things in order. I somehow managed to keep my composure as I received this devastating news and told Kara, *"Only God knows how much time Daddy has and when he would call him home."* After hanging up the phone, I took only three steps on wobbly legs and fell to my knees. *I cried out to God, "I don't understand! You just gave him back to me and now you're taking him away."* I clearly heard the Lord speak to my spirit, *"My child, it is not for you to know the times nor the seasons. I have given to you what you asked, time with your father while he yet lives, and you still have time. And you will have eternity with your father. I did not send you back home for your father, I sent you back home for your mother."*

I felt an overwhelming joy fill my soul as I received the promise from God that *I will have eternity with Daddy.* At the exact same time I was filled with great pressure at the thought that God was revealing his intent concerning Daddy's wife. I thought to myself, of all the people who walk this planet, *why me?* This woman hates me! I had *learned* from past experiences, it would do no good to argue with God. The correct *response* to this revelation should have been *why not me? God knows more than I of why me.* I just needed to submit and obey. I also knew that whatever God's plan—it would be what is best for everyone involved. I remembered and spoke out loud God's promise's to me—in your weakness, I am strong—lean on me, I will hold you up—I will never leave nor forsake you, and on and on the promises of God filled my mind. I then told my husband, who helped me deal with the flood of emotions I was experiencing. With God in me, and Jay by my side, *I was able to stand and started praising God for his mercy and love.*

Psalms 145:13–15: "Thy kingdom is an everlasting kingdom, and thy dominion endureth throughout all generations. The Lord upholdeth all that fall, and raiseth up all those that are bowed down. The eyes of all wait upon thee; and thou givest them their meat in due season."

Sometimes our burdens seem more than we can bear, and we wonder how we can go on. The psalmist stands at this bleak intersection of life's road and points toward the Lord, the great burden bearer. God is able to lift us up because he is great beyond discovery. God does mighty acts across many generations. He is full of glorious honor and majesty. God is righteous, gracious, compassionate, patient, merciful, and his love reaches out to us with tenderness. God remains close to those who call on him and listens to our cries. If you are bending under a burden and feel that you are about to fall, turn to God for help. *God will lift you up and bear your burden.*

It is here at this point that I believe I should take a moment to inform you, that I started writing this book when God started returning the memories of my personal family unit. As you recall I did not remember or even have any thought of my parents until I met and started interacting with Jay's parents. This area of my life had not yet unfolded. In the original manuscript I spoke of my parents as harshly punishing me for my weakness. And I spoke of Jim, the father of my children, as confessing to me how all the negative things that had happened in my life unfolded just as he had planned. I got to a certain point in the writing when I was asked by God to stop and wait. I obeyed and a time frame of three years unfolded before God told me to complete this book. Everything in the first manuscript was true, but without details. This book would still had been completed, but with a different ending. Only God knew ahead of time how this season of my life would be fulfilled. We all have choices to make as we travel through this life experience. Those choices produce the outcome—to the good or to the bad. God has given us free will and we are to freely and willingly choose him. Your purpose in life is to glorify God with your life. When you do this then you will hear, "Well done my good and faithful servant, enter into my rest." I quote a wise woman with this statement, "Life is a test and we must all travel through some monies, but in the end you have a testimony." You will understand why I told you this now, rather than later, as you continue to read.

Wait upon the Lord and His Timing

God has blessed my life by allowing me to receive some revelation of his will through dreams and visions. By positioning myself in continually communication through prayer with the Lord, I then receive understanding of the spiritual interpretation of the dream or vision. This is an amazing gift and requires great responsibility on my part in the areas of discipline and self-control. When God has made you aware that a certain event is about to unfold, waiting on his timing to release that information is one of the most difficult challenges in my life.

At this time in our lives, Jay and I had the opportunity opened unto us to enter into a college level teaching environment on the Word of God. We had already prayed and believed we had received the approval from God to continue in our spiritual growth in this manner at this level. We had acquired the recommendation statement from our pastor and had attended the orientation meeting. At orientation many requirements were addressed. The main focus and words spoken were, "If you are taking this course just to be able to say I accomplished it, you will struggle through it and upon graduation all you will have is a piece of paper to hang on your wall. This is a very difficult course, yet at the same time, it will be a life-changing experience. For every one hour of class, you will need to be dedicated to many hours of personal study time. The only way to accomplish this course and receive the full potential, depth, and benefit of its context is to be led by the Holy Spirit of God. This is only done by obeying the Spirit and applying these principles to your own personal life as you go through it."

After orientation my husband and I continued to pray. Because of the years of separation and receiving the recent news of my daddy's terminal cancer, the desire in my heart was now to spend as much time with him as possible. To get more insight and wisdom on this situation, Jay and I talked with our pastor. Informing him briefly of the details he gave this analogy, "If you are about to go to a certain destination, look at the clock and realize you will be caught up in rush hour traffic, is it not better to stay right where you are and avoid the frustration of being trapped in a stand still traffic jam. You can stay in the comfort of your home, wait one hour until rush hour is over, and arrive at your destination at exactly the same time. The decision and choice is yours. What kind of mood do you want to be in when you reach the destination? Frustrated and angry or good and peaceful!"

Together, we agreed it would be better for all, to wait. Pastor offered—Jay and I accepted a class that would require only one night, two hours of class time per week. Making this wise choice allowed us to remain balanced in life while attending to the many other responsibilities we faced daily.

Isaiah 40:31: "But they that wait upon the Lord shall renew their strength; they shall mount up with wings as eagles; they shall run, and not be weary; and they shall walk and not faint."

Waiting upon the Lord is expecting his promised strength to help us rise above life's distractions and difficulties. We all need regular times to listen to God. Listening to God helps us to be prepared for when he speaks to us, be patient when he asks us to wait, and trust him to fulfill the promises found in his Word.

Waiting for God to work does not mean sitting around doing nothing. I called Kara several times requesting permission to be involved in the medical process Daddy was going through. I asked,

"Can Jay and I please come visit and spend time with Daddy and you?" Kara continually denied my request stating, "I am going through a lot right now, I don't know how I will make it without your dad, and I don't want to be bothered with you right now. Maybe later, but not now!" Everything she said was all about her. What about the feelings and emotions others who love Daddy were experiencing? I honestly wanted to reach through the phone and slap the crap out of her! Can you feel my frustration? *Do you now understand why I said, "Waiting on God's timing is one of the greatest challenges in my life!" God knows this truth about me and in faith, I thank him that I have already overcome this weakness. We must do what we can, while we can, as long as we don't run ahead of God.*

While I waited to see how God would work in the situation, I continued to do what I could. I sought God's guidance through prayer and fasting and got things organized in my personal life. I also completed the original manuscript of this book. I finished with one of my favorite and most often used verses to encourage myself. *Philippians 4:13*: "I can do all things through Christ which strengtheneth me."

I was grateful for all God had already done for me but I still felt discontent. I had this empty space inside of me that I felt could only be filled when Kara would stop fighting against me and allow me to spend time with my dad. So much time had been wasted and so little time remained. I needed to stay focused on what I have, not on what I didn't have. To find true contentment in this situation, I need to change my priorities. I need to see with a different perspective and relay on my source of power. *Trusting completely on God's promises and Christ power will help me stay content.*

Acts 1: 7–8: "It is not for you to know the times or the seasons, which the Father hath put in his own power. But ye shall receive power, after that the Holy Ghost is come upon you: and ye shall be witness unto me."

Romans 8:28: "And we know that all things work together for good to them that love God, to them who are the called according to his purpose."

It was not for me to know *when* God would fulfill his promise toward me. And it was not for me to question *how* God would work His plan through me. *I was to trust his word and be ready to obey immediately.*

Around three months had passed since I heard the news of the Daddy's cancer (the doctors gave him six months) so of course I *figured Kara had no intention* of allowing me to see Daddy again. *But God* intervened! *Trusting* in God's timing works! The phone rang and it was Kara. She said, "Your father doesn't believe me. I told him I told you about his cancer but he said he doesn't believe me. Will you please tell him, that I told you?" In the background I could hear Daddy yelling at Kara, "You got her on the phone?" "Yes, Don, she on the phone." Turning the conversation back to me Kara continued, "I told your father that you have been working and that's why you haven't been by to see him yet, but I did tell you about his cancer, didn't I?"

Wow, what a spot to be in. God, Jay and I knew the truth! She was twisting the truth (and very good at it, I might add) to make it appear like I didn't care and that other things were more important to me than Daddy. (A half-truth is the same as a lie.) To Kara I said, "Yes, you did tell me about the cancer, but I would like to see Daddy and you. How about meeting us at the steak house Daddy suggested a while back for that Mother and Father's Day dinner I promised." We agreed, and reset a date and time. This time the meeting took place.

To the meeting I brought an encouragement card signed by both Steve and I. The words on the card said everything Steve and I felt in this moment. (How God will build bridges and reconcile people when time and distance has separated you from someone you love very much.) I also brought the first manuscript of this book. Placing them into Daddy's hand, Kara reached out and grabbed them saying, "I will need to read them to him because he can't see." Daddy drew back his hand and agreed saying, "Kara, will read them to me later." Doubting this would happen I said to Kara, "Why don't you read the card now, while we wait for dinner." Kara started to object, but Daddy said, "Yes, read it now." Kara reluctantly opened the card and read it, stopping at the signature, at which time I retrieved the card from her hand and stated, "This card is from both of your children, me and Steve. Daddy, do you remember your firstborn son Steve?"

"Yes I remember Steve, how is he doing?" "Steve is doing well," I replied and continued, "He knows about your cancer and wants to see you." Kara interrupted and stated, "Well, that's-not-going-to-happen!" While looking at Kara with painful and pleading eyes, Daddy replied to me, "Maybe later." I responded, "You don't have much time left to waste Daddy, you need to make a decision soon." I continued talking nonstop about Steve's life and what had taken place since they had last seen each other thirty-five years ago. I told of his military service, his medical condition, and his physical and spiritual life. At this point Daddy interrupted this one-sided conversation and said, "You and your brother are okay, your mother and I had you baptized when you guys were babies." I then explained the difference between being christened and being baptized. I explained to Daddy that Steve and I are okay because of what Jesus did for us, not for what he did or did not do. Our decision to ask Jesus into our lives is a personal choice that only Steve and I could make. I also talked about my life and how difficult it was growing up without a strong father figure. I talked about his amazing grand and great-grandchildren lives and how blessed they would have been, had they been given an opportunity to know him. I allowed the Holy Spirit in me to speak the correct words into my father's spirit with gentleness and love. Daddy listened intensely to every word and although he made no verbal reply, his body language displayed conviction and remorse for not being a part of our lives. "*We all love you and want you to know, there is nothing you have ever done that could make us love you any less or any more than we do today.* We love you and want to be a part of the life you still have been given by *God.*

I then told Daddy what the Spirit of God said to me the day I received the news of his cancer, "My child, it is not for you to know the times nor seasons. I have given you what you asked, time with your father while he yet lives, and you still have time, and you will have eternity with him. God does not lie to me. God will do what he promises." Looking at Kara and taking her hands into mine, I continued, "God also said, he did not send me back home for Daddy, but for you. You are about to go through the most difficult thing in this life you have ever experienced. Being separated from your husband, no matter how short of time it may be, will be painful. Let me help you."

Kara had not said one word during this whole one-sided conversation with Daddy. (That by the way is a work of God, a great miracle.) Kara and I just looked at each other, both with tears in our eyes. We both love the same man—she his wife, and I his daughter. In that moment there was a heartbreaking connection. (I had already experienced the pain of being separated from him and she was very soon going to experience that same pain.) *Many people use the cliché what goes around comes around. The Word of God says you will reap what you sow. How true is God's Word?*

Breaking the silence Daddy spoke, "So you and I will have eternity together. Tell me this, when we get there, will you let me do some of the talking?" We all laughed. We continued talking for hours about many less serious things, finished dinner, and returned to our cars. As Jay was putting Kara's wheelchair in their car, I noticed several tootsie roll wrappers on the floorboard and started to make a comment. Before I was able to say anything, I saw Daddy put his finger to his lips to silence me. Kara also saw this quick movement and also saw the candy wrappers. "Don," she said and continued, "you know you're not supposed to be eating chocolate." Smiling at me, Daddy said, "She is always worrying about me." Kara said, "I just love you and I'm watching out for you." I winked at Daddy and said, "You taught me better than that. If you're going to sneak chocolate, at least hide the evidence." Daddy and I had a good laugh as we made the "love of chocolate" connection. I saw a genuine love relationship between Kara and Daddy. They both worshiped each other. Kara was extremely insecure at the idea that anyone else could possibly love her husband as much or more than she does. Therefore, she eliminated that threat, by removing the relationship. Daddy simply accepted that unhealthy behavior, so not to hurt his wife. Therefore not preparing her ahead of time for the "what ifs" in life. God made all people unique and in general all people offer uniqueness into a relationship that nobody else can offer. I believe the root issue of all the division and broken relationships in this family unit is few had experienced the true unconditional love of God. *The first commandment of God is—There shall be none before me. When you make God first, all else will fall into place.*

I thought about the manuscript Kara now had in her possession and would soon be reading. Everything written within those pages pointed to Jesus and his transforming power in my life. I also thought about the fact that the details of my kidnapping, rape, and my life of prostitution, captivity, and bondage were also in those pages. I quietly pulled Kara aside and asked her not to read that part to Daddy. I did not want to add to the guilt he already carried inside himself for not being there for me when I needed him most. As I released that personal information about my life to Kara, she smiled, laughed and said, "I'm already aware those things happened to you." Those words hit me like a ton of bricks. I had never told anyone of those facts except my husband. Kara continued saying she agreed with me that Daddy never needed to know what had taken place in my life.

Since everything at that meeting ended well I truly excepted things in the future would unfold with much more ease. This however was not the case. Due to lengthy discussion I'm going to fast forward through the next two years. Yes, I know, although the doctors gave Daddy only six months, he lived an additional two years. (God is gracious and good, and knew ahead of time how things would unfold.) Daddy continued to work daily, and at the times when I was allowed to see him, he appeared more physically healthy than he did in the beginning. He gained weight and lost little to no hair at all. Chemotherapy and radiation made him tired, nauseated, and cold, but he never lost the brightness in his eyes, his smile or his sense of humor. I got this information about Daddy's condition from Ann, Bobby's wife. I had to communicate with her because Kara would not keep me informed, nor did she allow Jay or I to visit on a regular basis. Although I requested to visit weekly, I was allowed and received one visit every six months. (More than likely, when my father requested her permission to see me.) *I took full advantage of those cherished moments.*

Months had passed and Father's day was just around the corner again. I call Saturday requesting permission to spend time with Daddy on Sunday after church. Kara told me they planned to spend the day at the lake, they would be out of phone range, so I should not even try calling. Not being allowed to see Daddy on Father's Day broke my heart and I bawled my eyes out. Kara had surely tested me over and over again. I had pretty much reached the end of my patience with her. The word of God says, I will not test you beyond what you are able to bear, so I daily reminded God that I was no superhuman. *I had many conversations with God and had to repent several times for raising my disrespectful voice and speaking in words that were not very spiritually mature.*

In spite of Kara's request not to bother calling, I still tried several times but she never answered. God embraced and comforted me throughout the day with moments of laughter, smiles and good times with Jay, my children, grandchildren, and friends. Late that afternoon while in the process of picking out the perfect Father's Day card, my phone rang. Kara told me they had not gone to the lake after all and instead had a family gathering since this would probably be Daddy's last Father's Day. She continued saying, "Since everybody that came was her side of the family (which, as you recall, is the only family I ever knew) she figured I would much rather spend time elsewhere. Your dad asked why you and your husband were not here? I told him you guys were busy, have to work, and have families of your own. I promised your father I would call you and ask you to come over for a visit. If you guys can't make time I understand and will explain that to him, just let me know." Because we already had dinner reservations with Jay's daughter, I told Kara, *Jay and I will always make time for Daddy and we would be over tomorrow.*

I was now teaching monthly at church and weekly at Bible study. There is only one truth and that truth is based on God's unchangeable Word, yet God has allowed the teachers of his word to have their own personalities and has gifted his children with a variety of talents and skills to be used in delivering his message. Breaking down an important principle or concept to a level of understanding for the receiver is a skill I developed during my years as an educator of young children. I often use parables or short stories to incorporate the main point of the message. At the visits with Daddy, *I always brought the gospel message with me.*

At one of the visit's I taught on the great need to forgive. I read scripture, used examples and explained how important forgiveness of others applies to our personal lives today. Daddy took the information in, asked several questions, and understood the explanation I provided. Kara often made distasteful comments, for example, in the area of forgiveness she blurted out, "Your father and I don't need any type of forgiveness." Remaining calm, I asked, "Why do you believe that?" In a matter of fact voice, she replied, "Because we are good people." "Most people believe they are good people," I responded and continued, "but many good people don't go to heaven for eternity." Using body and sign language as I continued to speak I explained, "When you stand before the throne of God, as everyone of us will, you and you alone will have to give an account of your life. We have all made good and bad choices in life. Our advocate, Jesus will be there and our enemy Satan will be there. Satan will be accusing us of all the things we have done wrong, and what he says will be true. We do deserve to go to hell. But God sent his Son Jesus to redeem us, therefore, believers who have trusted in his finished work at the cross will be covered because of what Jesus has done for us.

Daddy started talking about his past, about his shortcomings and weaknesses, and about all his family he had not seen in years. Daddy asked Kara several times to help him remember the names of some of these people. Kara said, "Don, I don't know what you are talking about, you are just confused!" Frustrated Daddy yelled back at her, *"I'm not confused, I've just forgotten."* Using Daddy's words I quickly agreed, *"You're absolutely right, Daddy, you have just forgotten, who you are in Christ!"* Returning the conversation back to the original topic I continued saying, *"There is a good place to start, ask God to forgive you for forgetting who you are in Christ!"* "That's just absurd," Kara said and continued, "We don't need to ask God for that or any other type of forgiveness." Looking at Kara I frankly stated, "Only a fool would think they don't need forgiveness." Returning my attention back to Daddy, in the same tone of voice I continued speaking, "And what about your son Steve? Bobby is not your only son. You have three children. Your seed formed three children. Bone of your bone, flesh of your flesh. You and you alone will be asked, what have you done for my Son Jesus? Is it well with the souls of those I entrusted to you? How will you know what to say unless you make the connection and forgiveness is accomplished between the two of you while you are still here? Mom made mistakes also and Mom asked for forgiveness years ago and has been greatly blessed by God for doing so." (I speak the truth, I am out of the boat and walking on water in this moment. I had been told by Kara to never mention my mother and certainly never to call her Mom.) *I knew my words were not my own, but that of the Holy Spirit, because they were coming out of my mouth with boldness and confidence.*

Daddy then asked, "And how is your mother?" "She is well," I replied and continued, "She asked God to forgive her, took full responsibility for her part, and never spoke one negative thing to Steve or me about you. And she told me if you ever ask about her to tell you this—thank you for the time we spent together and thank you for our beautiful children. And she said to also tell you this— there is no weapon formed against her that shall prosper and she will see you again soon! You know, Daddy, forgiving Mom was easy for me because of her honesty. But I want you to know that someone did tell me a terrible lie about you! I started searching for you before my wedding day because I wanted you to receive the honor of walking me down the aisle. I call 358-#### and the voice on the other end told me I was too late, and that you were already dead." Raising my voice I continued, "How dare a voice on the phone tell me you were dead. I don't listen to no voice on the phone, *I listen to the voice of God—He told me you were alive and He told me how to find you.*"

Jay, who had been sitting by my side and had not said anything up to this point began talking. He talked of some areas in his life where he had made some bad choices and said, "If I knew then what I know today I would not have made the same choices, but I can't go back and change them. All I can do is learn from them, go forward, and choose never to make them again." I also shared about some of my weaknesses and quoted scripture, *"It is written, there is not one, no not one, save Jesus Christ, who has not sinned."*

Silence fall upon our conversation and Jay broke it saying, "Well, that was good, I need some fresh air, anyone care to join me?" Daddy took Jay's invitation and together they went outside. This left me alone in the room with Kara. As soon as the door shut, a very agitated Kara repositioned herself in the wheelchair and stared me down. Her eyes scoped me up one side and down the other. (It was obvious she knew something was different about me. I was no longer the scared child, she had controlled for so long. Inside I was changed, but she had no understanding of who had changed me.)

Because of past experience, I expected a voice filled with rage to come from her mouth. Instead she began to cry and her body began to shake with fear. In a voice of a scared, lost little child she said, "Help me, help me, I'm so scared." Somehow I remained amazingly calm (although, I'm sure my facial expression displayed shock with eyeballs as big as soccer's). I questioned, "What are you afraid of?" "It's your father, I fear for my life because of your father." "What are you talking about? What has Daddy done?" "He yells and screams at me all the time. And the other day while he was outside he was looking up to the sky, shaking his fist in the air and screaming at the top of his lungs and nobody was there. He is going crazy!" In a voice full of concern, I responded to Kara's words saying, "I have never ever seen Daddy do anything to cause you or anybody else harm! He is more than likely shaking his fist at God and blaming God for his life. Daddy is realizing that his life is near over and he has many regrets. It is not uncommon for someone to blame God when they reach this point in life and discover they have wasted much of it. *God understands. Daddy will be fine."*

"You don't understand!" Kara yelled and continued, "Your father tried to set this house on fire, while I was still inside it." Concerned by her statement, I questioned, "What are you talking about?" "Yes, Yes," nodding her head, she continued, "he poured gasoline all over the deck. I smelled the gas and asked him what he was doing. 'Are you trying to burn me alive?' He laughed and told me he was getting ready to wash the deck. I told him, that's not water but gasoline. The only one that saved my life was my grandson, who came and stopped him. I'm afraid to be alone with him. *I fear for my life.*"

I did not have time to respond to these words because Jay and Daddy were returning. As soon as the doorknob started turning Kara instantly repositioned herself in her chair, stopped shaking, put a smile on her face, voice became calm and started talking about what they were going to have for dinner. "*Wow!*" I thought to myself, could anything be more spooky than what I just witnessed? As Jay and I left the house that day I searched the deck, grass, and ground for any visible sign of spilled gasoline and I smelled the air for any strong odor. I found none. Jay asked me what I was doing. I said, *"I'm still trying to wrap my head around it myself, I will tell you on the way home."*

Jay and I knew that we were being used by God here in the physical realm, as partakers of a spiritual battle taking place in the unseen heavenly realm. Although we know this to be a true fact, throughout the next year, there were many spiritual battles that took place in which it appeared God had abandoned us and we also know, that was not true. For example, Daddy had requested to attend a family reunion, reconnecting with family he had not seen in over fifty years. He asked permission to attend our church to see a drama Jay and I were in, and to visit our home. He asked to be allowed to reconnect with son Steve, in which several different times arrangements had been made. On the scheduled day of these events Kara called and said they could not make it. All these and many more desires of Daddy's heart went unfulfilled. *Even though Jay and I had no understanding of why things did not unfold in ways we thought God would work, our responsibility was to trust and obey him. And to the best of our ability we did so.* Jay and I stayed in continual prayer. We sent our prayer request out to the worldwide mission fields that we actively support, and shared the situation with our spiritual leaders, who in turn, encouraged the entire church to pray. *The words chosen were short and to the point: (1) Daddy accomplishes all that God purposed him to do in this life. (2) Salvation for his wife. (3) Reconciliation to first-born son.* During this time frame both Steve and I received amazing blessings from God—both physical and Spiritual. The spiritual growth that took place in our lives cannot be explained in my own words, so I chose to use God's words!

1 Corinthians 13:4–7: "Love suffereth long, and is kind; love envieth not; love veunteth not itself, is not puffed up, doth not behave itself unseemly, seeketh not her own, is not provoked, thinketh no evil; rejoiceth not in inequity, but rejoiceth in the truth; beareth all things, hopeth all things, endureth all things."

God's kind of love is directed outward toward others and utterly unselfish. This kind of love is only possible when God helps us, so that we can give love while expecting nothing in return.

Genesis 50:19–21: "And Joseph said unto them, Fear not: for am I in the place of God? But as for you, ye thought evil against me; *but* God meant it unto good, to bring to pass, as it is this day, to save much people alive. Now therefore fear ye not: I will nourish you, and your little ones. And he spoke kindly unto them."

In the Bible, in the book of Genesis 30–50, the life of Joseph unfolds and ends in victory. During Joseph's life, his brother's convinced their father a wild animal had killed him, when the truth was they had in fact sold him into slavery. Joseph experienced several difficult situations while in captivity—Potiphar's wife's false accusation, the butler's neglect, and seven years of famine. Molded by pain and combined with a personal knowledge of God, Joseph survived and prospered where most would have failed. In God's perfect timing Joseph had the opportunity to forgive his brothers and treated them kindly in spite of their deliberate acts of evil against him. Joseph learned that God brings good from evil for those who trust him. Do you trust God enough to wait patiently for him to bring good from the bad that happens to you? *You can trust God, because as Joseph and I learned, God can transform evil to good.*

The physical blessing Steve and I received from God came in the form of money. Unexpected things began to happen in our lives that freed up our financial responsibilities, therefore, allowing us both to save. We had no understanding at the time of why this was taking place in our lives and decided to just rejoice in the fact that it was happening. Today, it makes perfect sense. Please continue to read and I will tell you why.

After a long awaited visit with Daddy in which I shared the gospel message and again talked about reconnecting with Steve, Kara told Jay and I to never return. She said, "It's hard enough that I have to watch your father dying, but for you to continue trying to convince him he needs to see Steve before he dies is unacceptable for me." Kara had been right by Daddy's side during each visit and had heard the same words of truth spoken. Daddy received the words and Kara rejected them. Jay and I returned home and *continued to pray, wait, trust and obey.*

I had a dream: Struggling to stay afloat on a raging sea was a large ship. The anchor of the ship was deeply buried in the muddy bottom. Huge waves were crashing down on the ship's deck and rocking it back and forth threating to turn it upside down causing it to sink. Several small tugboats surrounded the ship and started casting ropes upon the deck. After several failed attempts the ropes take hold, the tugboats pull, and the anchor breaks free of the muddy bottom. Seen off in the distance is a lighthouse on a hill, and the tugboats head in that direction. Around the base of the hill are many sharp rocks, but the tugboats see the narrow opening around the rocks and start going through it. I then wake up.

I asked God for understanding. The large ship represents a person with great power. The anchor buried deep represents the stubborn harden heart and the unwillingness to obey. The several tugboats represent the many people who love the large ship and are willing to help. The several failed attempts of casting the ropes represent the determination of the people helping to not give up. Upon the release of the anchor, the tugboats head in the right direction (toward the lighthouse, Jesus). However, there are many sharp rocks that represent many distractions and possible dangers. The narrow opening through the rocks offer great hope and represents (your choice) the one and only way to the lighthouse.

Two weeks had passed since Kara told us not to return again. I had tried many times by phone contact, only to received voice mail with no returned call. Other family members kept me informed of Daddy's cancer progression. I was made aware that Daddy was forced to stop working due to his fast failing health condition and had at last sat down to rest.

One morning Jay had gone to do some errands while I stayed home to do some house cleaning. I put the CD of Mandisa on, turned the volume up so high it shook the windows and played overcomer, over and over again. As I vacuumed, dusted, and did the laundry and dishes, I danced and sang at the top of my voice. The words of the song, I'm an overcomer entered into the very depths of my soul. I knew God was instructing me to return back to my parent's house even though Kara had told me not to. *I prayed. I cried, "Help me Lord!"*

In the Bible I marked all the scriptures the Spirit informed me ahead time I would need to accomplish what he was asking me to do. Both physically and spiritually dressed and armed I sat down and waited for my husband to return home from his errands. Meeting him at the door and quickly helping him put away the items his had purchased, I said, "We are to return today! Right now! I can't think about it or I may talk myself out of it!" *The truth is, when going into any spiritual battle to face the giant in your life, the greatest enemy is your thoughts about yourself. You must hold onto the strength and courage God has provided and move immediately.* Out loud I said, "As David ran toward Goliath and as Queen Ester ran toward the king, so I run, if I perish so be it." My husband understood my words, agreed with me and said, "I'm right by your side, supporting you all the way through!" Although I already knew I had his support, hearing his words gave my determination to win this battle an extra boost of courage. Ten minutes from our destination Jay turned our vehicle into the parking lot of a church (we had used this same parking lot at every visit in the past) and prayed. Asking the Holy Spirit to have complete control over our words and actions, therefore removing our own feelings and emotions from the situation. *We arrived, knocked, turn the knob of an already unlocked door, entered in and loudly announced our arrival.*

From the living room, Daddy's happy but very weak voice responded, "I'm here, come on in!" From the bedroom Kara said, "I told you guys not to come without calling first, it's a miracle we are even home." In my mind I thanked God for already having them separated in different rooms and loudly said, "Jay is going to spend time with Daddy, I came to see you. Stay right where you are, I'll find you!" In the seconds it took me to locate Kara, she was already getting up from bed and trying to get into her wheelchair. Seeing this I quickly ran to help her. Steadying her against a possible fall I put my arms around her and with boldness gently said, *"I mean you no disrespect by not asking your permission first,"* paused, repositioned myself to where I made eye contact with her and continued, *"but I am a child of God. I listen to and obey his voice and his voice will always trump yours!"*

Taking a deep breath I continued to talk nonstop for about an hour. I spoke of all the written and many unwritten things this book contains. How difficult it was for me to forgive her, and how difficult all areas in my life were until I discovered the healing power and love of God. I reminded her of my ten years of complete long-term memory loss and how today I thank God for those years. Because it was during that time frame I personally experienced God's mercy, grace, and love toward me. Kara did not speak one word as I shared with her the horrific things I had experienced prior to my salvation. And that after salvation several more years passed before I made the personal connection. Kara appeared unmoved and unconcerned about my past life situations including the detailed description of the kidnapping, rape, and years of bondage and captivity.

Following the leading of the Holy Spirit, I then told her of an occurrence that had taken place in the life of my daughter where God ahead of time revealed to me in a dream that something was about to unfold. Because of the intensity of the dream, urgency to inform my child filled my soul, I made contact with Renee, told her the context of the dream, the spiritual meaning, advised and encouraged her to take the necessary steps to protect herself and family against the attack. Two weeks later my child experienced a home invasion in which robbery was the main intent. Her husband got his wife and child into the safe place and ran for help, even though he had been shot twice. Tony (my daughter's husband) was taken to the emergency room with life-threating wounds. The bullet in his stomach had penetrated a large precancerous tumor, in which may never had been discovered had this home invasion not occurred. One year later this family unit are alive and well, and the intent of the evil plotted against them (to take the lives of my son-in-law, my child, and my grandchild) went unfulfilled and in fact, by the discovery of the unknown tumor, saved Tony's life. We don't understand why God choose this way to make the tumor known to us, but we are grateful for his love toward us. *God's ways are not our ways.*

Kara may not have shown interest in the words of God, but she was intrigued by the spiritual revelation and understanding I received through prayer concerning dreams and visions. Having her interest peaked, I then told her the dream I had received about the large powerful ship and small tugboats and explained the spiritual implications. I then paused and allowed Kara an opportunity to respond. She simply replied, *"I have always been afraid of drowning."* I then opened the Bible and read the scriptures I had previously marked concerning salvation. Kara said, "I'm already saved." She then told me why she believed her words to be true. I told her, "Many people think they are saved because they speak the words of salvation and are baptized. Many people receive the good news of the gospel and then make the unwise decision to stay in their sins because that way of life has become comfortable for them. Many people chose not to obey the instructions or commandments of the Lord found in his word, therefore many people do not grow up spiritually and in time become disconnected from their source of power. When you study the word for yourself you will receive knowledge, have understanding, and truly believe in your heart the words of salvation spoken to be true. This will produce and inward transformation and an outward change in your decisions, attitude, behaviors, and actions. And based on your own words and actions there is *no evidence* that this transformation has taken place within you. Only God knows the condition of the heart and he knows the attitude, the intent, and the motives of the heart. *Let's pray together and make sure you are connected and saved."*

The Holy Spirit prayed through me and Kara repeated the words. Kara showed no visible emotion but I welcomed her words, "I have never before felt like I did as you prayed with me, it feels like the weight of the world has been lifted from my shoulders." "Amen." I said in agreement with her words. It is common for me to express great rejoicing toward the person in whom God has allowed me the privilege of leading to him. I normally would extend my hand, shake their hand and say, "Welcome to the Kingdom!" Instead out of my mouth came this question, "I wonder who and why someone on the phone would tell me my father was dead?" Kara shrugged her shoulders and said, "I have no idea who would say such a thing to you." Righteous anger filled me and out of my mouth came, *If I know it was you, know for a fact God knows it was you!"*

Upon returning home, in private I talked with God about my angry emotions. The conversation was lengthy but in general I said, "Why Lord? I obey and do as you ask of me. At the very least I expected some tears. At the very least I expected to hear her say, I'm sorry. At the very least I expected some sort of repentance to take place. But noooo, instead she looked me square in the face and continued to lie. And what thanks do I get for doing your will? Now I get to spend eternity with her!" I clearly heard the Lord firmly respond, *"My child, this is for my glory, not yours!"* God's right. I'm wrong. No more needed to be said. I then received this thought, "Buy for Kara a good study Bible." I did this, went back the following week, handing it to Kara while saying, *"This is your lifeline to God. You must do your part—seek him, know him, and you will find that in him, there is forgiveness for your sins. You will find true life like you have never before experienced. God loves you more than anyone else has every loved you. That is God's promise to you and God never lies."*

Kara's eyes flooded with tears and she said, "If God forgives me and if God loves me, then tell me why my life is so miserable?" She then proceeded to tell me how her son had informed her and Daddy of his plans, to have an estate auction and sell everything they owned, including their home. This was a curveball that God had not prepared me for. I asked many questions of my own and for the most part I believe Kara told me the truth. I discovered she and Daddy were upside down financially in their mortgage and had several unpaid debts to numerous locations. Utilities were about to be shut off and she was not certain of where their next meal was to come from. I told Kara not to worry, I promised her I would do my part to help, and God was in control of the outcome.

I asked her what Bobby's plans were for caring for Daddy while he is here and his plans for her after Daddy's gone? Kara said, "Bobby told me to trust him." I reassured her that God already knows of this situation and God already has a plan for her life. I then told her again to read the Bible, to start in the Gospels, and get to personally know the Son of God, Jesus. I said, *"You will never be able to trust Bobby to care for you, if you do not first trust the Son of God to care for you. And you will never believe what I tell you to be true, if you do not first believe every word of the Bible to be true."*

The first thing was to pray and receive guidance from God. I then contacted another family member who was aware of the financial status of Daddy's estate. He informed me that years ago Daddy had bankrupted his business, paid cash for the property they live on today and planned to enjoy the remainder of his life in retirement. Due to Kara's uncontrollable spending habits, Daddy had to continue working and providing for not only her, but for extended family members as well. I was heartbroken at this news but no matter how Daddy had arrived at this point in his life, I was determined to do what I could to help. I live in a different state than Kara and Daddy so I spent several hours by phone getting familiar with their state laws concerning helping the aging and disabled. Daddy was a veteran, so I contacted the Veterans of America concerning possible housing. Explaining the emergency circumstance in which Kara, physically disabled, and the terminal illness of Daddy, Red Cross and many other organizations offered help. As I mentioned earlier Steve and I had been blessed financially and we both had savings. I talked with Steve concerning taking care of Daddy in his last days and without any hesitation Steve said, *"I want to do whatever I can do to help."* *"Wow."* God gave me an amazing brother with a big, big heart in Steve. Although Kara had forbidden him to spend any time with Dad and he needed help himself, Steve was willing to do whatever he could to help another in need. With the help of others and together with my brother Steve, we managed to keep the utilities on and agreed to pay them monthly until further notice. Due to the legal requirements concerning a veteran with a terminal illness, the Veterans of America were unable to help with housing. Kara found an assistance living facility in which she would be welcome and Jay and I agreed to pay the moving cost.

During the next few weeks Jay and I were allowed to visit with Daddy as often as we liked without requiring Kara's permission first. Before the estate auction, Kara asked me, "Would you be willing to pay for a storage bin so I can save some of our personal items?" "Yes, I'm willing to do this for you," I responded and continued, "*we all have personal treasures in this life that we hold dear to our heart, however a wise person will treasure and save that which is dear to God's heart. There are only two items within the walls of this house that are more precious than rubies, more valuable than gold to God. And that would be your and Daddy's souls.*"

I then shared the gospel message I had prepared for Sunday morning with Daddy and Kara. The theme and main point of the message is—*God holds people accountable for unrepented sin. How God in his love and mercy toward his children gives several opportunities to repent and receive forgiveness of our sins before judgment, and how God in his grace always provides a way of escape.* The Bible Scriptures used in this message was Genesis 9:1–2, *God rescues Lot.*

Two angels had been sent by God to wicked Sodom to locate and remove Lot and his family prior to total destruction. The two angels find Lot sitting at the city gate, a place of authority indicating a position of great status. Lot invited the angels to stay within his home and showed hospitality toward them. Before nightfall, strangers from the city knock on the door, demanding Lot to send the angels out to them so they could engage in sexual relations with them. Lot refused but offered his daughters instead. This terrible suggestion reveals how deeply sin had been absorbed into Lot's life. Instead of using his godly knowledge to shape the environment, he had allowed his environment to shape him and became hardened to evil acts. Lot had lived so long and so content among ungodly people that he was no longer a witness for God. Abraham, Lot's uncle, pleaded and prayed for Lot's life——God was merciful and saved Lot from the fiery death that engulfed Sodom. However, Lot hesitated when the angel seized his hand and rushed him to safety. He did not want to abandon the wealth and comfort he enjoyed in Sodom. Clinging to the comforts of the past, unwilling to turn completely from sin, Lot's wife died when she turned back to look at the smoldering city of Sodom. *You can't make progress with God as long as you are holding on to pieces of your old life. Jesus said it this way in Matthew 6:24: "No man can serve two masters."*

After the estate auction, I asked Bobby how he did financially. He said, "I did better than I thought I would, but I was not able to sell the house. It should sell soon though." I did understand why Bobby made the decision of the estate sale, but I give no respect concerning his timing in the matter. While terminal cancer was eating away at Daddy's physical body, the emotional stress of seeing everything you have built your life around being sold to the highest bidder while you're still alive is in my opinion, extremely disrespectful. Bobby's decision to sell the house would also make his family in need of a new home. Without Daddy's financial help, the house could no longer be supported. The chaos, confusion, tension, and division within the atmosphere of the house became overwhelming for even a healthy person. It was very painful for me as I saw my daddy suffer in this way, so I continued to encourage him in the comfort of knowing, for him the pain would be over soon.

Upon request, hospice service removed my daddy from his home atmosphere and placed him into their facility keeping him comfortable during his last two weeks. Kara stayed with him daily and Jay and I continued to visit weekly. At our last visit there, several others from Kara's side of the family had also come to visit Daddy. Those present had all been born during my time of separation from the family, therefore they knew nothing about my past or the pain I had experienced. I welcomed the conversation, as they sat around talking about the great memories they had shared with my daddy. This behavior was healthy and appropriate until Kara noticed I was smiling and nodding my head with approval.

Kara suddenly turned all her attention on me and said, "Yes, yes we have had such great times with your father." Then going back and forth between the others and me, Kara taunted and mocked me, sharing stories and saying, "It's too bad you missed out on all these great times." I was filled with rage toward Kara, but clearly heard the Spirit within me redirect my thoughts, saying, *"She has no power over you!"*

Immediately filled with overflowing courage, I found the common ground in the conversation with the young people and boldly said, "Didn't you guys say you are school teachers?" "Yes, we are," they affirmed and I continued, "I was a teacher to young children for twenty-five years. Isn't it amazing how much love you can have for children that are not even your own?" On this common ground, laughing we started talking about the innocence of children in all the silly things they do and say. And how *as responsible teachers, with love guiding us, we are able to redirect their negative behaviors into a long-term positive outcome.*

Kara became very uncomfortable, looking at the clock and questioned, "Don't you have somewhere you need to be?" Doing a visual search of the room with my eyes and not seeing her Bible anywhere, I quickly responded, "Going to see Steve when we leave here. We plan to share with him the message I gave this morning, but I'm sure he will be thrilled to know I shared it with you and Daddy first. *It's about God's grace!"*

As I gave the message one by one the others excused themselves and left, leaving only myself, Jay, Kara, Daddy, and of course the Holy Spirit's presence in the room. Preparing to leave also I kneeled by Daddy's side, talked a few more moments about God's grace, kissed him on the forehead and said, *"I love you, Daddy, see you again soon."*

Daddy gently took me by my hand and in a very weak voice whispered, *"Tell Steve I will see him at my new home."* I reassured Daddy that Steve loved him very much and that he would in fact see Steve again. As I looked at Daddy's physical body for the last time I noticed the white hair he had lost during his cancer was growing back and in process of turning black, I thought to myself. *Thank you God, for allowing me to see these amazing things, you're totally awesome.*

Upon returning home, I again asked God why the desire of my heart went unfulfilled—Daddy and Steve being reconciled in this physical realm. God revealed to me, his pleasure in me for my persistence in prayer concerning this area. His love for Steve by not exposing him to more pain in the area of rejection and assured me that Daddy was not held accountable for things he had no understanding or control over. In helping me to remain steadfast God spoke these words into my Spirit, *"There are many things happening in which you have no understanding and are unable to comprehend at this time."*

Psalms 41:1: "Blessed is he that considereth the poor: the Lord will deliver him in time of trouble."

The Bible often speaks of God's care for the poor and his blessing on those who share this concern. God does not want the poor to suffer, but rather God wants our generosity to reflect his own free giving.

Four days later, from a family member, I received the information of my daddy's passing. *I rejoiced in the fact that Daddy is no longer suffering.*

Ecclesiastes 3:1–2: "To every thing there is a season, and a time to every purpose under the heaven: A time to be born, and a time to die; a time to plant, and a time to pluck up that which is planted."

God provides the cycles of life, each with its own work for us to do. God breaks down the barriers and gives to us opportunities to discover for ourselves that only God is the lasting solution to life's disappointments and problems. *The secret to peace with God is to discover, accept, and appreciate God's perfect timing.*

Kara and I had not made contact since my last visit with Daddy, nor had she contacted me concerning his passing. I did however receive a call from her concerning financial help in paying for the funeral arrangements.

Together Jay and I agreed to cover this need, provided the account number of my charge card to the funeral director and requested Kara to inform us of the date and time. Three days later, Sunday morning before Communion, I prayed and asked God to examine my heart and remove any evil or sin I may be unaware of. I then asked God to give me confirmation that my daddy was home with him. In my mind, I saw Daddy sitting at a picnic table located beneath a large oak tree. His hair was thick, wavy, jet black and blowing in the breeze and his body was healthy, strong and completely healed. Daddy was eating on something chocolate, a cupcake I believe. An overwhelming strong love emotion drew me toward him. As I approached, Daddy extended his hand that held the cupcake and said to me, "eat." At that moment I put the Communion into my mouth and started eating.

Jay saw this and questioned, "What are you doing? It's not time yet!" Surprised myself, I blurted out, "Daddy told me to eat, so I ate." I then whispered in Jay's ear what God had just done. Daddy's laughter had always been contagious to anyone who had been blessed to know him. With this thought on my mind, I whispered in Jay's ear, "Just like Daddy to mess with me like that." Out of respect for the Lord's Supper, we tried but somewhat failed to contain our laughter during the remainder of the Communion. As we left the sanctuary and enter the hallway, we discovered tables lined with rows of chocolate cupcakes donated to the church for the people to enjoy. *"Wow!" What an amazing God we serve.*

Having a sense of urgency fill my soul, Jay and I cut the fellowship opportunity short and hurried to our jeep. Once inside I checked the phone for missed calls and discovered I had I received a voice mail from a concerned family member stating, "Where are you and Jay? The funeral is about to start. I asked Kara did she tell you guy's the date, time, and place. She said she told you. I believed her. I'm so sorry, please forgive me, I should have made sure for myself. I hope you get this message in time. The funeral is at the church where your dad was a member. Hurry, it starts in two hours."

The other missed call and voicemail was from Kara, it simply said, "Call me." Both calls had come in just moments before and were only five minutes apart. Jay and I were over and hour drive away from the church Daddy had attended, so as Jay drove in that direction, I made phone contact and informed others. These others' were the immediate family members of both Steve and my family—Daddy's grandchildren and great-grandchildren. Because of the short notification only Judy, Ashley, Jay, and I were able to meet the timeline and attend.

Approximately ten minutes from the church my phone began ringing nonstop displaying Kara's name and number. I deliberately avoided answering, opting instead to ask God to keep my spirit peaceful—contain my anger and control my tongue. When I did answer Kara said, "Have you lost your mind? I did call you over and over again. You never answered." Maintaining a calm voice I responded, "I have my phone with me right now, there is not one missed call or any message from you until this morning after I was informed by someone else about the date, time, and place. Only then did I receive a voicemail from you stating, 'call me.' There were no details, nothing more, but it is okay, Jay and I will be there soon." I then proceeded to tell Kara the events that had taken place earlier that morning and how God had confirmed to me that Daddy is in heaven with him. When I finished speaking, Kara simply said, "That's great."

Upon arrival at the church many of Kara's family members were present, remembered me as a child, embraced and welcomed both Jay and I. There was still a little time remaining before the funeral was to start so we had small conversation with many people. Many told me that Kara had informed them of my accident involving the head injury and said, "Cindy is very confused in the mind and not to believe anything I might say." I reassured them that God had healed and restored my mind. I shared the truth about Steve's mental condition and the circumstances surrounding my return back home after so many years. Like me, most had cut family ties due to Kara's behaviors, but also like me, loved my father very much and felt the need to reconnect. I spoke with the pastor, who knew nothing of Daddy's personal life and was completely unaware that Bobby had an older sister and brother. I assured him both Steve and I loved our father and have only good things to say about him. Bobby approached and broke into the conversation saying, "Ya, my older brother Steve is a nut case." Ignoring what had been said and making eye contact with the pastor, I continued, "Some people only believe what they are told and never take the steps to discover the whole truth for themselves. As I was saying before Bobby interrupted, many of Daddy's last wishes went unfulfilled but as you can see for yourself God has other plans, for here I am," pointing to Judy and Ashley, I continued, "and they are here representing Steve, Daddy's firstborn son. The uninvited guest of Kara, *are the invited guest of God.*"

The funeral was about to start, everyone took their seats—Kara, Bobby, and his family sat in the front—Jay, I, Judy and Ashley chose to sit a few rows back with the friends of Daddy. The pastor spoke first then opened up the pulpit to family and friends to share with others their memories of Daddy's life. Bobby spoke first—we were not raised in a Christian home, and Dad was a good man. Bobby then shared a couple of good times he had with Dad growing up and stepped down from the pulpit.

As surely as the Lord lives within me, I tell you the truth. *God moved my body.* I felt myself stand and being move forward, *before* I realized I was walking. As I walked forward and up the steps to the pulpit, I loudly introduced myself, "I am Cindy, daughter of Don Johnson." Suddenly Kara shouted, "Get her off the stage." Bobby immediately obeyed Kara's demand. Quickly turning, running across the pulpit toward me, while loudly proclaiming, "NOW IS NOT THE TIME."

"What are you doing?" I asked. "Now is not the time," Bobby repeated over and over again. As Bobby overpowered me, shoving and dragging me down the steps, I went from surprised to confused and into complete shock within moments. I said, "When is the right time to say something good about Daddy?" Trying to regain my footing, Bobby continued pushing me toward the door, insisting I leave the church. My husband came around the corner and demand, "Get your hands off my wife!" Refusing to loosen his grip on me, while responding to Jay, Bobby yelled back, "Let's take this outside." Jay then took hold of Bobby's tie, twisting it and cutting off his air supply, thus loosening his grip and allowing me to break free. Jay then said to me, "Come on, Cindy, it's time to leave." Submitting to Jay's request, I followed him outside.

Police cars pulled into the lot. Extending my hand as I walked up to the officers, I said, "My name is Cindy, I am the reason why you have been called here today." As I explained the situation to the officers, many relatives of Kara's came outside and told the officers I was telling them the truth. Bobby is about four times my physical weight and had tossed me around like a rag doll, so I had several bruises already starting to appear. Seeing these and believing what they had been told, the officers asked if I wanted to press assault charges against Bobby.

I responded, "No good would come of that, besides I have already forgiven him. Bobby was just reacting to his mother's words and doing what he believed to be right." Bobby does not know what Kara knows—that I was sent back by God to help her. Before I arrived here today, because of her disrespectful behaviors, I asked God to give me confirmation on what he wanted me to do concerning Daddy's widow. I never expected to get physically plowed down by my little brother. *"I intend to do what the Word of God says, if you are not welcome in your own home, you are to shake the dust from the sole of your feet, hold your head up high and keep on moving forward."*

On the drive home, I started laughing and asked Jay, "What took you so long to come to my rescue?" Also laughing Jay said, "Man, it took me a minute to wrap my head around it. That is the most bizarre thing I have ever seen at a funeral. Your dad's in a much better place and after this performance we have no reason to feel obligated to helping his wife out any more. Do you agree?" "I've already deleted her number from my phone," I responded, but inside I struggled with the idea of deleting Kara from my heart. Things had taken place that I had not been prepared for. Why had God not prepared me for the possibility of complete rejection and the public humiliation I had just experienced? Had it not been God, who had sent me back home with the message of forgiveness and reconciliation? What about the verse, do unto others as you would have them do unto you? I had experienced great pain in my life due to the rejection and abandonment of Kara and Daddy during the time when I needed them most! Was I not now doing the exact same thing to Kara, as she had done unto me? Inside of me, this was an awful feeling! *Inside of me, I felt shame and guilt for not successfully being the peacemaker I believed God intended for me to be! Inside my heart, I truly felt like I had failed God in the assignment he had given me!*

Feet Firmly Planted and Standing on the Righteousness of God

I have enough knowledge and understanding of the Word of God to recognize that the confusion I was feeling in my spirit and experiencing in my mind and heart was not of God. Satan is a very real being and an enemy of God and all God represents. As a representative of God, even alert and spiritually aware mature Christians can let their guard down and become a vulnerable target to the attacks of Satan.

On the same day of Daddy's life celebration, I received a call from Ashley who had decided to remain at the funeral of her grandfather. She said, "When I got up to speak, I also was told I was not allowed to say anything. After the funeral, my mom spoke with Kara about her treatment toward anyone connected with Dad or you. Kara said, 'Of all days, I do not want to hear anything about Steve or Cindy. What about me? This day should be focused on me, I was Don's wife!' "Not a good wife." Judy had replied."

Ashley told me, she and her mom have already deleted Kara's number from their phones and decided to have no more contact with that side of the family. I told Ashley I had done the same. I told my children what had taken place and all three said the same thing, "Had we have been there, we would have helped Jay defend you Mom. Nobody is allowed to put their hands on you and live to talk about it!" I admire my children for their concern toward me and at the exact same time, I thanked God for unfolding his plan as he had so my children were not present when the attack against my character occurred.

I then spoke with my little sister, Michelle. With her I can share the emotional part of the experience and receive wise feedback. As I spoke she continued to interrupt, asking me to repeat certain details of the event. I could tell by her shocked tone of voice, she was going through the moments with me in her own mind. When I finished, she asked, "Why do you think God allowed this to happen to you?" Without any hesitation I replied, *"Because God is preparing me for greater things!" "Absolutely,"* was all she said. *"Wow,"* I thought to myself, *"thank you God for giving me a little sister to share your wisdom with."*

At the same time I was receiving encouraging words from people who knew and loved me, I got a disrespectful text message from one of Bobby's children demanding I apologize to her grandmother for causing a disruption at grandpa's funeral. Knowing she did not understand, I made no response. In hope Kara would acknowledge her poor judgment and course of action I did respond and returned a missed call from Kara. "Sorry I did not hear the phone ring but see a missed call from you, do you want to talk about something?" I said and waited for a response. When I received none, I continued, "I strongly advise you to read your Bible. Within those pages, you will find yourself and you will have understanding of why your life is as it is." I hung up the phone and cried. It was in those words spoken to Kara that I realized I needed to take for myself that wise advice. *I opened my Bible and asked God for direction.*

Psalms 37:23: "The steps of a good man are ordered by the Lord: and he delighteth in his way."

A person who follows God, trust him, and tries to do his will. When you seek his advice, God watches over and directs every step that person takes.

James 1:1–2: "My brethren, count it all joy when you fall into divers temptations; knowing this, that the trying of your faith worketh patience."

The depth of our character is revealed when we see how we react to a situation while under pressure. We are to turn our hardships into times of learning, and see them as opportunities for growth.

Matthew 10:16–23: "Behold, I send you forth as sheep in the midst of wolves: be ye therefore wise as serpents, and harmless as doves. But beware of men: for they shall deliver you up to the councils, and scourge you in their synagogues; and ye shall be brought before governors and kings for my sake, for a testimony against them and the Gentiles. But when they deliver you up, take no thought how or what ye shall speak: for it shall be given you in that same hour what ye shall speak. For it is not ye that speak, but the spirit of your Father which speaketh in you. And the brother shall deliver up the brother to death, and the father the child: and the children shall raise up against their parents, and cause them to be put to death. And you shall be hated of all men for my name's sake: but he that endureth to the end shall be saved. But when they persecute you in this city, flee ye into another: for verily I say unto you, Ye shall not have gone over the cities of Israel, till the Son of man be come."

As Christ's disciples, we are not to be sheep-like in our attitude but sensible and prudent. We are not to be gullible pawns but neither are we to be conniving. We are to find a balance between wisdom and vulnerability to accomplish God's work. Living for God often brings on persecution, not only from without (governments and courts), but also from within (friends and family), but with it comes the opportunity to tell the Good News of Salvation. Jesus told the disciples that when arrested for preaching the Gospel, they should not worry about what to say in their defense—*God's Spirit would speak through them.*

Colossians 4:6: "Let your speech be always with grace, seasoned with salt, that ye may know how ye ought to answer every man."

Enduring to the end is evidence that you are truly committed to Jesus. Persistence is a by-product of a truly devoted life. Many people ask as I do, "Why Lord does justice against those who take advantage of others appear to go unnoticed?" Jeremiah expressed these feeling in

Jeremiah 12:6: "For even thy brethren and the house of thy father. even they have dealt treacherously with thee; yea, they have called a multitude after thee: believe them not, though they speak fair words unto thee."

God doesn't give Jeremiah a doctrinal answer; instead he gives a challenge—if Jeremiah can't handle this, how will he handle the injustices ahead? Not all of God's answers to prayer are nice and easy to cope with. Life for Jeremiah was extremely difficult despite his love and obedience to God. When we call for justice, we must realize that we ourselves would be in big trouble if God gave each of us what we truly deserve. Any Christian who has experienced bereavement, war, abuse, rejection, abandonment, or a serious illness knows this.

Christ however, warned the disciples against premature martyrdom. They are to leave before the persecution got to great. We have plenty of work to do and many people to reach. We are to be committed to God even when the going gets tough and when his answers to our prayers don't bring immediate relief. Our work won't be finished until Christ returns. And only after he returns will the whole world realize his true identity. There are times in life where you must make the decision to separate yourself from others for your own spiritual safety. Make sure you are following the leading of the Holy Spirit in your decision. *The Bible has many testimonies of people who have traveled this road before you. How awesome it is to learn valuable lessons in life by examining what history has already taught.*

About one month had gone by since my daddy's passing. I received the statement of the charge card in which I had used to cover his funeral expenses. I discovered there were several items charged to the card beside what I had agreed to. I made contact with both the funeral home and the storage bin concerning the charges. Both places told me, Kara told them to charge the cost to the number already on file. I explained the situation, agreed to cover what I owed, and requested receipts. While taking care of this matter, I asked the funeral director for information concerning Daddy's memorial. I was told to his knowledge, Daddy had no memorial in place and his ashes belonged to his wife. I said, "No disrespect intended but Daddy's ashes belong to God. There are many people who loved my daddy and were not allowed to be a part of his life without first receiving Kara's approval. Nobody should have to be subject to requesting Kara's permission to visit his memorial." The funeral director agreed but legally he had to obey the law.

Because Daddy was a veteran, the director suggested I contact Veterans of America. Being already actively involved and familiar with the VA policies due to their connection with Steve, and recently with Daddy's housing situation, when I requested an honorable home-going and memorial for him the VA said it would be a privilege. I was told as long as I provided the proof and identification of my relationship to Daddy, it made no difference how many years may pass or if I ever receive his ashes, they would provide this service and give him a marker, therefore allowing anyone at any time the opportunity to visit his resting place. Today, I am content with carrying the memories of Daddy in my mind. *And in my heart I believe and wait on God for that day of celebration in the future.*

Mark 11:23: "For verily I say unto you, That whosoever shall say unto this mountain, Be thou removed, and be cast into the sea; and shall not doubt in his heart, but shall believe that those things which he saith shall come to pass; he shall have whatsoever he saith."

Another bizarre event that took place was receiving an envelope address to and from myself. Inside I discovered Kara's unpaid and past due bills. On the bill she had scratched out her name and address, and wrote in care of my name and address. At first I simply disregarded this behavior as ignorance and made no response. The next month however I gave this matter deeper thought. Through the mail I was now receiving statements directly from Kara's service providers with my name and address on them, and I was getting junk mail in my maiden name. (Cynthia Johnson, a name I had not used in over thirty years). I was suddenly receiving preapproved loan applications in my name and phone calls from collection agency's requesting Kara's connect information. To prevent further harassment, I made contact with the bill collectors. Giving the account number provided on the bill, I was assured they would no longer send the debts my way. I thought about the possibility of Kara acquiring access to my social security number through her marriage to my father. I notified a security service that helps in the prevention of identity theft activity. Life lock will monitor and contact me immediately should anything suspicious take place. Having my identity secure I then thought on the spiritual significant of the situation.

Romans 13:14: "But put ye on the Lord Jesus Christ, and make not provision for the flesh, to fulfill the lust thereof."

When we "put on the Lord Jesus Christ" we exemplify the qualities Jesus showed while he was here on earth (love, humility, truth, service). In some sense, we role-play what Jesus would do in our situation. Only life experiences and maturity through time help to put people in a position of hoping, believing, and trusting in Jesus. I knew I must not give into my fleshly emotion and desire of making personal contact with Kara. Expressing my frustration toward her, therefore giving opportunity of opening the door to gratifying her sinful desires toward me. I also knew that if I interfered in God's natural order of things as they unfolded, I could possibly hinder God's plan for Kara's life. Ignorance is not to be an excuse for sinful living and the love of money is the root of evil. Kara wrongly assumed that money could be exchanged for God's free gift of healing and mercy, and I could not be ignorant of what God was asking of me to do. To find answers, it is always wise to ask yourself, *"What would Jesus do in this situation?"* John 7, Jesus encounters conflict with religious leaders, gives a clear example of what Jesus did do in my situation. This chapter shows the many reactions people had toward Jesus. They called him a good man (7: 12), a deceiver (7: 12), a devil-possessed man (7: 20), the Christ (7: 26), and the Prophet (7:40).

John 7:3–5—Jesus's brothers had a difficult time believing in him. Some of these brothers would eventually become leaders in the church, but for several years they were embarrassed by him. After Jesus died and rose again, they finally believed. We today have every reason to believe because we have a full record of Jesus's miracles, death, and resurrection. We also have the evidence of what the Gospel has done in people's lives through the centuries.

John 7:7—Because the world hated Jesus, we who follow him can expect that many people will hate us as well.

John 7:10—Jesus came with the greatest gift ever offered, so why did he often act secretly? The answer—because the religious leaders hated him and would refuse his gift of salvation no matter what he said or did. The more he taught and worked publicly, the more these leaders would cause trouble for Jesus and his followers. So it was necessary for Jesus to teach and work as quietly as possible.

John 7:13—The religious leaders had a great deal of power over the common people. It was apparent that they couldn't do much to Jesus at this time, but they threatened anyone who might publicly support him. Excommunication from the synagogue was one of the reprisals for believing in Jesus (John 9:22). *John 7:13*—Everyone was talking about Jesus! But when it came time to speak up for him in public, no one said a word. Jesus says that he will acknowledge us before God if we acknowledge him before others (Matthew 10:32).

John 7:16–19—Those who attempt to know God's will and do it, will know intuitively that Jesus was telling the truth about himself. Jesus's followers should do more than the moral law requires, by going beyond the do's and don'ts to the spirit of the Law.

John 7:20–23—Most of the people were probably not aware of the plot to kill Jesus (John 5:18). There was a small group looking for the right opportunity to kill him, but most were still trying to decide what they believed about him. While the religious leaders allowed certain exceptions to Sabbath laws, they allowed none to Jesus, who was simply showing mercy to those who needed healing. We must make up our own minds about who Jesus is, knowing that whatever we decide will have eternal consequences.

John 7:40–43—The crowd was asking questions about Jesus. Some believed, others were hostile, and others disqualified Jesus as the Messiah because he was from Nazareth, not Bethlehem (Micah 5:2). But he was born in Bethlehem (Luke 2:1-7), although he grew up in Nazareth. If they had looked more carefully, they would not have jumped to wrong conclusions. When you search for truth, make sure you look carefully and thoughtfully at the Bible with an open heart and mind.

John 7:44–46—Although the religious leaders had authority over minor civil and religious affairs, controlled their own temple guards, and gave the officers power to arrest anyone causing a disturbance, these officers couldn't find one reason to arrest Jesus. And as they listened to him to try to find evidence, they couldn't help hearing the wonderful words he said.

John 7:50–52—Nicodemus risked his reputation and high position when he spoke up for Jesus. His statement was bold. Nicodemus confronted the Pharisees with their failure to keep their own laws. The Pharisees saw themselves losing ground—with their hypocritical motives being exposed and their prestige slowly eroding, they began to move to protect themselves. Pride would interfere with their ability to reason, and soon they would become obsessed with getting rid of Jesus just to save face. What was good and right no longer mattered; they continued to break their own laws by plotting to kill Jesus.

The temple guards came back impressed by Jesus (John 4:16), and one of the Pharisees' own, Nicodemus, was defending him. This is the last time Nicodemus is mentioned in Scripture, but tradition says he was baptized by Peter and John and later forced to step down from his position as a member of council.

We may condemn our predecessors (religious leaders) for their failures, but we are twice as guilty if we repeat the same mistakes that we recognized as failures. Often we are so ready to direct God's message at others that we can't see how it touches our own lives. After studying John 7, I was forced *to examine my own heart*

Isaiah 42:18–22: "Hear, ye deaf; and look, ye blind, that ye may see. Who is blind, but my servant? Or deaf, as my messenger that I sent? Who is blind as he that is perfect, and blind as the LORD'S servant? Seeing many things, but thou observest not; opening the ears, but he heareth not. The LORD is pleased for his righteousness' sake; he will magnify the law, and make it honorable. But this is a people robbed and spoiled; they are all of them snared in holes, and they are hid in prison houses: they are for prey, and none delivereth; for a spoil, and none saith, Restore."

How could I be God's servant and yet be so blind? How could I be so close to God and see so little? Had I not failed in the same way? Sometimes in partial blindness-seeing but not understanding, or knowing what is right but not doing it---which at times can be worse than not seeing at all. We must humbly remember our position before the incomprehensible, holy, and eternal God. *Only God knows if and when his creation will respond to him. We must recognize that God's ways are best*

Acts 26:15–18: "And I said, Who art thou. Lord? And he said, I am Jesus whom thou persecutes. But rise, and stand upon thy feet: for I have appeared unto thee for this purpose, to make thee a minister and a witness both of these things which thou hast seen, and of those things in which I will appear unto thee; Delivering thee from the people, and from the Gentiles, unto whom now I send thee, To open their eyes, and to turn them from darkness to light, and from the power of Satan unto God, that they may receive forgiveness of sins, and inheritance among them which are sanctified by faith that is in me."

This verse is a reminder that *all* have opportunity to an equal share in God's inheritance. This inheritance is the promise and blessing of the covenant God made with Abraham (see Ephesians 2:19; 1 Peter 1:3, 4).

Isaiah 30:18, 20: "And therefore will the LORD wait, that he may be gracious unto you, and therefore will he be exalted, that he may have mercy upon you: for the LORD is a God of judgment: blessed are all they that wait for him. And though the Lord give you the bread of adversity, and the water of affliction, yet shall not thy teachers be removed into a corner any more, but thine eyes shall see thy teachers."

The Lord gave his people the bread of adversity and the water of affliction, but he promised to be with them, teach them, and guide them during hard times. God demands a lot from us, and many times following him can be painful; but he does this out of his love for us. When you go through a difficult time, try to appreciate the experience and grow from it, learning what God wants to teach you. God may be showing you his love by patiently walking with you through adversity.

During the first fifty years of my life, I had always felt like I needed to be the peacemaker in all circumstances and often I would take *false responsibility* for the situation at hand. As spoken of in the previous chapter, I felt like I had failed God in completing the assignment he had given me to do. Inside of me, *this produced a false sense of shame and guilt.*

Romans 12:2–3: "And be ye not conformed to this world: but be ye transformed by the renewing of your mind, that ye may prove what is that good, and acceptable, and perfect, will of God. For I say, through the grace given unto me, to every man that is among you, not to think of himself more highly than he ought to think: but to think soberly, according as God hath dealt to every man the measure of faith."

Our refusal to conform to this world's values must go deeper than the level of behavior and customs; it must be firmly founded in our minds: "Be ye transformed by the renewing of the mind." (Only the Holy Spirit can renew and redirect our minds.)

When you think too much about your worth in the eyes of others, you could miss out on your true value in God's eyes. Healthy self-esteem is important—the key to an honest and accurate evaluation of ourselves is—knowing the basis of your self-worth—our identity in Christ.

Matthew 5:48: "Be ye therefore perfect, even as your Father which is in heaven is perfect. Christ calls all his disciples to excel, to rise above mediocrity, to mature in every area, becoming like him."

Ephesians 4:14–15: "That we *henceforth* be no more children, tossed to and fro, and carried about with every wind of doctrine, by the slight of men, *and* cunning craftiness, whereby they lie in wait to deceive; but speaking the truth in love, may grow up into him in all things, which is the head, even Christ."

Christ is the truth (John 14:6), and the Holy Spirit guides us in the truth (John 16:13). Satan, by contrast, is the father of lies (John 8:44).

Some Christians fear that any mistake they make will destroy their witness for the Lord. We see our own weakness, and when an individual stumbles, as I did, other Christians, family and friends, helped pick me up, and encouraged me to continue forward in faith. We must be committed to the truth, which means our words will be honest and our actions will reflect Christ's integrity. Speaking the truth in love is not always easy, convenient or pleasant; but it is necessary.

John 8:32: "And ye shall know the truth, and the truth shall make you free."

Jesus frees us from the consequences of sin, from self-deception, and from the deception by Satan.

Philippians 2:13: "For it is God which worketh in you both to will and to do of his good pleasure."

God has not left us alone in our struggles to do his will—we are to submit to His control and let Him do the work.

To be like Christ, we must condition ourselves to think like Christ.

Christians are to have the mind of Christ and to have Christ's desires. To do God's will, we need:

1. The power of the indwelling of the Holy Spirit (Philippians 1:19).

2. The influence of faithful Christians.

3. The obedience to God's Word (not just exposure to it).

4. And we need to operate in our life the sacrificial service to our Lord.

1 Peter 5:10: "But the God of all grace, who hath called us unto his eternal glory by Christ Jesus, after that ye have suffered a while, make you perfect, establish, strengthen, settle you. To him be glory and dominion for ever and ever. Amen."

After you suffer a while, God will complete the process—*why* suffer a while? *Why* not now complete the process? Let's take a deeper look at the character of God and allow His Word to fill our mind and answer these questions!

Deuteronomy 8:3, 5, 7, 9, 10: "And he humbled thee, and suffered thee to hunger, and fed thee manna, which thou knewest not, neither did thy fathers know; that he might make thee know that man doth not live by bread only, but by every word that proceedeth out of the mouth of the LORD doth man live. Thou shalt also consider in thine heart, that, as a man chasteneth his son, so the LORD thy God chasteneth thee. For the LORD thy God bringeth thee into a good land, a land of brooks of water, of fountains and depths that spring out of valleys and hills. A land wherein thou shalt eat bread without scarceness, thou shalt not lack any thing in it; a land whose stones are iron, and out of whose hills thou mayest dig brass. When thou hast eaten and art full, then shalt bless the LORD thy God for the good land which he hath given thee."

Many people think that life is based on satisfying their appetites. If they can earn enough money to dress, eat, and play in high style, they think they are living "the good life." But such things do not satisfy our "deepest longings." These things in the end leave us empty and dissatisfied.

Real life comes from total commitment to God, the one who created life itself.

A totally committed life to God, requires discipline, sacrifice, and hard work, and that is why most people never find it. As our friendship with God deepens, it leads to strength of character, peace of mind, and deep satisfaction.

So again: the question, *why* suffer awhile, *why* not immediate change? Answer—because after you do change—you will *know* it was God (and not done in your own strength). God is not mocked!

Remember; that the most valuable thing in life—your relationship with God—is *free! Only God knows the condition of an individual's heart.* Due to the circumstances that took place before, after and surrounding the death of my daddy, my heart was still deeply troubled. Although I had received encouragement from family and friends, and I truly believed God had spoken His instructions to me, *I still did not feel peace of mind* concerning the decision. Jay and I decided to take a two-week motorcycle road trip to reflect, relax and refresh ourselves.

This is an actual event that took place on the first day of our vacation, mid-July, in South Dakota. As normal practice we arose early, spent time in God's Word, eat a hot breakfast and talked of our daily plans. It was a beautiful, perfect morning. The sky was blue with not a cloud in sight. Jay watched the weather station, which said 20 percent chance of possible scattered showers in early evening. Jay and I reasoned, perhaps we would not need to carry with us the rain gear and body armor, after all we will want to buy souvenirs and we would need the space in our bags for our purchased treasures. And according to the time frame of the weather reporter, we would surely be back to the cabin before any rain may hit. A wise biker will always carry rain gear and body armor so after more consideration, Jay and I decided it was better to be safe than sorry and we made certain we had all the proper covering just in case of an unexpected weather change. Having all things in order, *we prayed, thanking God for this beautiful day, for giving us opportunities to tell others about Him and for returning us back home safely.*

Jay and I got on our bikes and headed toward our destination, one hundred miles away. We enjoyed the ride, taking in the beautiful surrounding and making brief stops at several key landmarks. Reaching our destination, we spent some time shopping, had lunch and decided we should start heading in the direction of our cabin. Jay looked at the map and discovered a different route, taking us along twisting and curving roads and through many valleys and hidden "hot spots" for bikers. We stopped at one of these "biker paradise hot spots" around 2:00 in the afternoon and fifteen miles from our cabin. Our plan was to hang out for an hour and get back home before any rain may come our way. In search of the perfect tee shirt, we entered a place named the Bumping Buffalo and decided to rehydrate ourselves with a cold drink. My husband ordered a drink called moose drool. Laughing I said, "Really, you're going to drink something called moose snot?" Jay replied, "It is not moose snot, it's moose drool!" Again laughing I said, "Well, moose snot or moose drool, both are moose body fluids and both sound disgusting to me." "Taste great," Jay said and continued, "I would have another, but we should think about getting back home before the rain starts." *I agreed.*

As soon as we walked out the Bumping Buffalo we noticed the temperature had dropped, the wind had picked up and clouds were filling the sky. Looking up, Jay pointed to the west and said, "Those

clouds have a greenish color, that means hail. We need to move fast."
We had beaten many storms in the past, so quickly moving forward
had become like second nature to both Jay and me. Had we taken the
time to look at the radar equipment that was attached to our motorcycles, *we would have made a different choice.* And had we prayed and
asked God for his wisdom on the situation, *we would have turned
around,* gone back into the Bumping Buffalo and had another moose
drool. (Jay and I did neither of these things, but instead chose to
think and believe we could out run the storm.) *Common sense*—
we are on the first day of a two week vacation—so what if we are
stranded in a really cool town for a couple of hours—we had plenty
of time and nowhere else we needed to be. Prayer, insight and God
given *Wisdom—would have planted us and we would have waited until
after the hailstorm had passed.*

Jumping on our bikes, we headed south, toward home. As we
left the valley, without the wind buffer of the buildings, the wind
steadily became more intense. A huge wind gust forced the motorcycle into the oncoming traffic lane. *Thank you, God,* there were no
vehicles at the time. On the left side of the road was a rock wall, on
the right side a steep cliff. There was no safe place to pull off the
road. The rain started, then turned to pea size hail, then to marble
size. Jay and I not taken the time to properly gear up prior to heading
into the storm, so we both had a lot of skin exposed. Needless to say,
marble size hailstones—hurt. I thought to myself, "*Thank you, God,
for keeping us safe.*" Instantly, off to the right was a gravel road. *Jay
and I pulled off.*

Our clothes were soaked and our bodies were bruised but we
were provided a place to stop. Thank you, God. And again I say,
"Thank you, God," as we removed our body armor and rain gear
from our saddlebags and covered our bodies. Where Jay and I were
located there was no physical shelter, so we positioned ourselves over
the tank of the motorcycle, facedown, hands under our chest, and
allowed the now quarter size hail stones to hit our backside and hel-
mets. As we waited for the storm to lighten up, emergency vehicles
speeded by on the road. I thought to myself, someone ahead of us
had not been as fortunate as Jay and me.

About twenty minutes later the storm did lighten up. Knowing we had only a short amount of time before the storm would resume, Jay and I proceeded forward slowly with caution in the direction of our cabin. About five miles up the road, we found ourselves in a standstill traffic jam due to an accident that had taken place. A short distance off to the left, Jay spotted a small information booth at the entrance of a state park. Motioning to the people in the cars surrounding us to allow us through, they moved, providing a small path, and we managed to maneuver our bikes out of the traffic jam.

When we reached the information booth, a man named Jim opened the door and welcomed us inside just moments before the hailstorm returned. Jim said he had witnessed the accident and had called 911. He had seen a couple on a motorcycle being pushed by the wind into oncoming traffic. Not knowing the outcome of the people involved in the accident, Jim, Jay and I held hands, *thanking God that these people did know Him.*

Over the next hour, several more bikers arrived at the booth. There was standing room only, but we kept crunching together, allowing one more to come in out of the storm.

One of the other bikers had come from the location Jay and I were heading. He showed us pictures on his phone he had taken of the area. The unexpected hailstorm had hit so suddenly and so hard that many people were stranded, the town was completely closed down, and snow removal equipment was being used to clean the streets of the golf ball size hail. In time, Jay and I were able to continue forward and return to our cabin safely.

All the vehicles, including our jeep had major hail damage. As Jay examined the damage to our jeep, he stated that only the hood appeared dented. This of course, was very frustrating for Jay because in the backseat of the jeep lie the dry and unused padded hood cover. We had purchased and brought with us this hood cover for just in case of such an emergency. We had listened to the weather report prior to storm. We had been misinformed. The good news is that we have insurance for such a situation. We decided, to not allow this unfortunate circumstance ruin the rest of our vacation. The remainder of our time was filled with good times and great memories. *God reveals himself through the storms in our lives.*

Upon returning home from our vacation, the following Sunday, I was to give the message. As I prepared the message I used the experience of the hailstorm as an example and the valuable lessons God taught me through the storm.

1. Only God knows the condition of each individual's heart, and due to the attack that had taken place against my character, I did not have peace of mind in how to continue forward.

2. Together, Jay and I agreed, time away from the pressure to reflect, relax, and refresh was needed. So we took a vacation.

3. As normal practice, we spent time with God, ate a hot breakfast, and made plans for the day.

4. As an extra effort, Jay listened to the weather report and I packed our body armor and rain gear.

5. We prayed, Thanking God for a beautiful day, opportunities along the way and returning us home safely.

6. We set a destination with an allowable time frame to accomplish our plans for the day and return home safely *before the 20 percent* possible scattered showers arose. Up to this point, Jay and I had done the right things. It is also at this point, where we discovered, God taught us some very valuable lessons in life.

7. We all are only human—people (weather reporters) often misinform us. Beware! People (teachers) of God's Word are only human, and can misinterpret scripture. Make the extra effort by taking the time to study scripture for yourself.

8. Do not make a hasty decision—Jay and I had the proper tools available to us to make a wise choice. (We had weather radar on the motorcycle, and plenty of time for prayer.) Be alert! When making a decision involving *common sense and wisdom*, use all tools provided. Be prepared ahead of time, by studying the Bible. And always take time to ask God for

His wisdom concerning any situation in life. He will always tell you what is best for you. *Obey Him!*

9. Pray continually in faith—when Jay and I found ourselves in an unsafe situation, I thank God for keeping us safe. (Note—*I did not ask God to make things safe for us, I thanked God we were already safe.*) Instantly I spotted the gravel road, where Jay and I were able to pull off, stop the bikes and put on our body armor and rain gear. When you know who you are in Christ, believe in things that are not, as if they are and speak those things out of your mouth, God will open your eyes to see things that you may have missed otherwise. *The most effective privilege children of the Lord have—is prayer.*

10. Always be prepared for an unexpected storm—*thank God* we did have our body armor and rain gear in our saddle-bags. Remember, that morning Jay and I had considered not bringing it with us on the trip. After more consideration, the statement was made, a wise biker will always be prepared for the unexpected. *A wise child of God will always cover themselves in the spiritual armor of God. The helmet of salvation, the breastplate of righteousness, the belt of truth, the shoes of peace and carry the sword at all times, which is the Word of God, written on your heart and always being ready to speak the Word out of your mouth in any situation.*

11. Pray for others—when Jay and I were trapped in a stand still traffic jam due to an accident that had taken place down the road ahead of us. *We prayed.* Our eyes were open to see the hailstorm had made a turn and was coming back toward us from the rear. *We prayed.* Our eyes spotted the small shelter. *We prayed.* People moved their cars, allowing a small path for Jay and I to get through and out of the traffic jam. *We thanked God, and prayed more.* When we reached the shelter, a man came out and invited us in out of the storm. *We thanked God and prayed* for the people involved in the accident. More bikers found their way to the safety of the shelter, we crunched together, making room for all. *We thanked*

God and continued praying. Some bikers showed us pictures of what lies ahead on the road we were traveling. *We thank God that we were covered, safe, and warm. And we stood still and waited until it was safe to proceed ahead.*

12. Be thankful for all things—when Jay discovered the damage the hail had done to our jeep, he was frustrated for a short time, because had we received the correct information in a more timely fashion, different decisions and choices would have been made, therefore avoiding the storm altogether. *The good news is,* we have insurance to cover the needed repairs of the jeep. After some reflection, we realized we had so much to be thankful for. Had things happened any other way, we would not have learned some very valuable life lessons and I would not have this story to share with you. Before I was saved, I thought "I going through life alone with no one to help me." *How grateful* I am today, to know I am not alone. I thank God for my life companion in my husband Jay. *And I thank God* for being with both of us as we travel the road of this life toward our eternal destination. No matter what storms in life may come our way, *we are able to remain strong and have complete peace of mind, because we have the assurance and know God is with us.*

Philippians 3:9–10 and be found in him, not having my own righteous, which is of the law, but that which is through the faith of Christ, the righteous which is of God by faith: that I may *know* him, and the *power* of his resurrection, and the fellowship of his *sufferings*, being made conformable unto his death."

When we are united with Christ by trusting in him, we experience the *power* that raised him from the dead. That same mighty *power* helps us to live morally renewed and regenerated lives. But before you can walk in newness of life, we must also die to sin (be "made" conformable unto his death). Just as the resurrection gives us power to live for him, his crucifixion marks the death of our sinful nature.

God had sent Jay and me back home to my parents to represent him. Through us, God had warned that money could not save them. No amount of trickery or hasty activity could speed up God's grand design. We must lay aside everything harmful and forsake anything that may distract us from being effective Christians.

I do have reason to feel sorrow about my past and for the way I was treated by many of Kara's relatives at Daddy's funeral. We all have done things for which we are ashamed, and we all live in the tension of what we have been and what we want to be. *Today, however, because my hope is in Christ, I can let go of that past sorrow, shame, and guilt, and I can look forward to what Jesus will help me to become.*

God Reigns.
Past, Present, Future

I dare not complete this book without giving an answer to a question that many of you may be asking, "What will happened to Kara?"

To be completely honest, only God knows! Let us examine scripture in this area.

Romans 3:22–24 "Even the righteousness of God which is by faith of Jesus Christ unto all them that believe: for there is no difference: for all have sinned and fall short of the glory of God; being justified freely by his grace through the redemption that is in Christ Jesus."

Some people believe certain sins are greater than other sins because of the obvious consequences are much more serious. Murder, for example, seems to be worse than hatred, and adultery seems worse than lust. But this does not mean that because we do lesser sins we deserve eternal life. *All* sin makes us sinners and *all* sin cuts us off from our holy God. *All* sin, therefore, leads to death (because it disqualifies us from living with God) regardless of how "big" or how "small" it seems.

"Justified freely" means to be declared "not guilty." All charges are removed from the record. When God forgives our sins, our record is wiped clean, as though we have never sinned. *The good news is—God's solution is available to all of us regardless of our background or past behaviors.*

At the writing of this book, six months have passed since I last had contact with Kara. I know that she actively has many family members in her life that love her. I know that God loves her more than anyone of these people and I know, by my own experience, *God is love.*

The family of God includes *all* who have believed in him in the past, all who believe in the present, and all who believe in the future. We are *all* a family because we *all* have the same Daddy, he is the source of *all* creation, the rightful owner to everything. *God promises his love and power to his family, the church.*

Ephesians 3:14–21: "For this cause I bow my knees unto the Father of our Lord Jesus Christ, of whom the whole family in heaven and earth is named, that he would grant you, according to the riches of his glory, to be strengthened with might by his Spirit in the inner man; that Christ may dwell in your hearts by faith; that ye, being rooted and grounded in love, may be able to comprehend with all saints what is the breadth, and length, and depth, and height; and to know the love of Christ, which passeth knowledge, that ye might be filled with all the fullness of God. Now unto him that is able to do exceeding above all that we ask or think, according to the power that worketh in us, unto him be glory in the church by Christ Jesus throughout all ages, world without end. Amen."

This has been my prayer for Kara, as well as for myself, and all others God places across my pathway. Before I knew God, God did know me, and I asked God to give to me the ability to love unconditionally. I thank God for answered prayer!

In the beginning God created me for a purpose. I did not understand or know what that purpose was. It is now my purpose to live out the rest of this life serving God in this generation. Living the rest of my life for the glory of God will require a change in my priorities, my schedule, my relationships, and everything else. It will sometimes mean choosing a difficult path instead of an easy one. Even Jesus struggled with this. Knowing he was about to be crucified, he cried out: *"My soul has become troubled; and what shall I say, Father, save* Me from this hour? But for this purpose I came to this hour. Father, *glorify Thy name."*

The Bible says, "For our light and momentary troubles are achieving for us an eternal glory that far outweighs them all." As God's child, I must wait for him in quietness and confidence. Today, I experience true love that could only be found in a solid relationship with Jesus. Today, my future is as bright as the promises of God.

Philippians 3:12–14: "Not as though I had already attained, either were already perfect: but I follow after, if that I may apprehend that which also I am apprehended of Christ Jesus. Brethren, I count not myself to have apprehended: but this one thing I do, forgetting those things which are behind, and reaching forth unto those things which are before, I press toward the prize of the high calling of God in Christ Jesus."

Revelation 22:12–13: "And, behold, I come quickly; and my reward is with me, to give every man according as his work shall be. I am Alpha and Omega, the beginning and the end, the first and the last."

Those who "do his commandments" are daily striving to remain faithful and ready for Christ's return. In a world of problems, persecution, evil, and immorality, Christ calls us to endure in our faith. Our efforts to better our world are important, but their results cannot compare with the transformation Jesus will bring about when he returns. He alone controls human history, forgives sin, and will recreate the earth and bring lasting peace.

Revelation 22:17: "And the Spirit and the bride say, Come. And let him that heareth say, Come. And let him that is athirst come. And whosoever will, let him take the water of life freely. Both the Holy Spirit and the bride, the church, extend the invitation to all the world to come to Jesus and experience the joys of salvation in Christ."

Romans 11:36: "For everything come from God alone. Everything lives by his power, and everything is for his glory."

Psalms 139:17, 18: "How precious also are thy thoughts unto me, O God! how great is the sum of them! If I should count them, they are more in number than the sand: when I awake, I am still with thee."

God's character goes into the creation of every person. His Spirit is ready and willing to work within you. He is thinking about you all the time. When someone you love is thinking about you all the time, it comforts you. God, the King of creation calls you his child.

How your life story ends, depends on choices you make as you travel through this physical realm. These life-changing choices will lead to destruction or victory—choose life, choose victory.

About the Author

Cindy and her husband Jay live in Kansas City. They attend Crest Bible Church and serve in the many areas of outreach provided through the motorcycle ministry. Each with their own motorcycle, they enjoy traveling throughout the beautiful countryside while taking the Gospel wherever God would send them. How awesome it is to do good for God's Kingdom, while journeying in a lifestyle that is a perfect fit. What a mighty God we serve!

Together they have four adult children, seven grandchildren, and are looking forward to many more.

Today and forevermore, living life in the victory of the risen *Lord* and Savior, Jesus Christ.

CPSIA information can be obtained
at www.ICGtesting.com
Printed in the USA
FFOW05n2117121217